SELLING is a CINCH

SELLING is a CINCH

Doug Malouf

How to become a successful salesperson in 8 easy steps

SIMON & SCHUSTER
AUSTRALIA

Acknowledgments

With anything I do a cast of thousands becomes involved. Some of the stars of this production:

Peter Geekie
Julian Hall, Project Manager
Janice Dawson
Kirsty Melville
Stephen Kocizki

and you, because you have been game enough to buy it.

Also by Doug Malouf
How to Create and Deliver a Dynamic Presentation

SELLING IS A CINCH

First published in Australia in 1990 by
Simon & Schuster Australia
7 Grosvenor Place, Brookvale NSW 2100

A division of Paramount Communications Inc.

National Library of Australia
Cataloguing in Publication data

Malouf, Doug.
Selling is a cinch.

Includes index.
ISBN 0 7318 0148 2.

1. Selling. I. Title.

658.85

Designed by Christie & Eckermann, Art and Design Studio, Sydney

Illustrations by Allan Stomann

Typeset in Oracle by G.T. Setters Pty Limited
Printed in Australia by Globe Press

CONTENTS

Author's Note

For me, selling is a way of life, a commitment to service and the customer.

At the tender age of seven I was selling red jellies, rock-salt and horseshoe nails from my father's general store in Canowindra, population 1600.

The professionalism required for successful selling has changed since those simple, innocent days. As competition has increased, consumer awareness has grown, and the demand for quality service has risen. To succeed, salespeople require a greater understanding of the selling process.

It is my firm view that a better seller is a smarter, well-read, organised and informed seller.

We are all involved in selling. In this book I have identified the path that must be taken in the making of all sales — the all important sales cycle.

There are eight easy-to-follow steps which I have endeavoured to present based on my years of selling experience. *Selling is a Cinch* is designed to simplify and demystify many of the unnecessary fears we hold and obstacles that we as salespeople often place before ourselves.

The selling techniques have been presented using colourful, entertaining examples in an easy-to-read format. Educating adults must be fun and exciting to be fruitful.

Remember to take each step of the sales cycle I've discussed with enthusiasm and determination. If you accompany the ideas and techniques in this book with persistence, you'll soon find out that selling really is a cinch.

Stay Positive

Doug

Foreword

Of success, Mark Twain wrote: 'All you need in this life is ignorance and confidence; then success is sure.'

The abundance of ignorance causes us to be unsure of how to utilise the lot we have. And, the lack of success we achieve, or we think we achieve, often leaves us bemused and concerned about making our dreams a reality.

This great 'hands-on' book that Doug has written takes hold of the success patterns needed to win in the selling profession—and explains them in a concise, simple manner.

If you are a newcomer to the wonderful world of selling, a journey through the following pages will give you some wins and successes that you may never have achieved. And, if you are already walking down a successful pathway, you will understand the value that one idea from this power-packed book could mean to your career.

Doug Malouf has done it all in the selling game. From start to finish, I have been impressed by the amount of time and effort he puts back into his profession, in helping others towards their achievements.

The publication of this book, and the impact it will have on those travelling down success road, will be another chapter in the life of the winning author. A chapter, perhaps headed: 'Life wasn't meant to be difficult. These steps will show you why.'

John Nevin.

Salesman—World Book Encyclopedia
Founder of SWAP Australia (Salesman With A Purpose)
Inaugural National President—National Speakers Association.

INTRODUCTION

The Sales Cycle

Selling is a basic part of life for all of us. It's a bit like love. Remember the old saying, 'Love makes the world go round.' Well, I also believe that selling makes the world go round. This book will show you how to effectively jump on the merry-go-round, stay there, and have fun at the same time.

Everyone is involved in selling in one way or another. The butcher, the baker and the candlestick maker all sell their products. They've been selling for years. Well, at least since I was a child! But it doesn't stop there: teachers sell ideas, preachers sell values, doctors sell their diagnostic and healing skills, waiters sell service. And it is easy to see from looking at your average politician that they are involved in selling themselves. If they're not, they usually don't get elected.

Unfortunately, there are some people in the community who regard a career in selling as a bit of a joke. You know the attitude: 'Some of my best friends are sales representatives, but would you let your daughter marry one?' Even some sales reps themselves are a bit ashamed of how they make their living. Now that's sad, isn't it? And it's especially sad because it's absolutely unnecessary. No matter what profession you're in, you should be positive and proud of what you do.

I can assure you that I've been selling all my life and selling is a career to be proud of. In fact, it was the renowned international public speaker Dr Ken McFarland who said that it is the great salespeople who really make things happen in the world. How can that be? Well, think about it.

Dr Gene McSplice, brilliant biochemist and genetic engineer, invents a miraculous new compound which, depending on where you apply it, cures baldness, enhances sexual performance or relieves the discomfort of haemorrhoids. Does this mean that Dr McSplice can confidently expect fame and fortune overnight? It certainly does not! The truth is that unless the good doctor discovers a salesperson who is able to bring this wonder drug to the marketplace, it will probably never get out of the laboratory. Great ideas only become effective if somebody sells them to the public. That's something to be proud of. It is for this reason that you should always remember the salesperson's famous comeback:

> 'Nothing starts to happen at all in life until somebody sells something to someone else.'

Now that's fairly important, isn't it? But there's more. If it wasn't for salespeople very little progress would have been made in the way we live. We'd still be reading by candlelight and fishing the toddlers out of the pit toilet. It isn't enough to develop the technology which allows progress to happen. People have to be persuaded to accept the new technology. It might seem obvious to us that it is better to read by electric light and not as messy to pull the kids out of the flush toilet, but people are conservative. They like things the way they are, and someone has to persuade them to act in their own interest before they'll change.

Dr McFarland tells a story about a young man, in the early years of this century, who was trying to sell the first horseless fire-engine to a town council in the United States. It looked easy. The old horse-drawn engine usually arrived at the scene of the fire in time to cool down the smouldering foundations of the demolished building. But the new engine was fast and efficient. It had all the latest firefighting equipment. It was obvious that it might actually save properties from burning to the ground. And wasn't that the idea?

Well, the young man went off to the council meeting full of enthusiasm. He told them about the new engine with conviction. His sincerity was obvious. He really believed in his product. He spoke convincingly and persuasively.

When he had finished, the town fathers looked at him seriously. Thank you, they said, it had been very interesting, but they liked things the way they were. The horses had been pulling the fire-engine for over twenty years and everyone knew what to expect when a fire happened: someone would sound the alarm and the horses would be saddled to the engine while the firemen got dressed in their uniforms and brass helmets. Then the race would begin. With its bells ringing, the engine would be dragged wildly through the streets by the team of horses, while the firemen, looking like ancient heroes, would cling desperately to the swinging waggon, their faces red with elation, or whisky, their axes glittering in their belts. Everyone knew there was a fire. The crowds would gather and follow on behind the engine, impressed and excited. Now, who in their right minds would want to trade such a spectacle for mere efficiency? Who would put human life and valuable property ahead of an important public ritual like this? In any case, the fire chief said, if the engine arrived in time to save the foundations that was reward enough, no-one expected more. The distinguished councillors nodded wisely. The chief was right, and besides, if a new engine was to be considered that would require a committee decision. That could take some time: months, perhaps even years. It was not something they wished to rush into.

Did our energetic salesperson become discouraged in the face of this set of minor objections? Fortunately he didn't. He just kept on selling and finally he succeeded. The town council bought a new fire-engine and a new era of effective firefighting began.

The point is, we are all better off because of the salesperson's persistence, and because he could see the way forward more clearly than those who were supposed to be older and wiser. It wasn't the manufacturer of the fire-engine, or even the inventor, who led the way, it was the person who sold the engine. He gave the council an alternative way for the future. A few more examples like this one, and we might see selling as the noblest and most important job of all.

Of course selling has changed over the years like everything else. The old creed in selling used to include the following proverbs of dubious wisdom:

'Tell 'em anything. Just sell 'em.'

'You must be a good talker to survive.'

'Start closing 'em as soon as you meet 'em.'

As we approach the end of the twentieth century, salespeople have to realise that these old ideas are as obsolete as horse-drawn fire-engines. There is a new breed of professional salespeople out there in the marketplace now. Selling is no longer the job you do when you don't have a job. It's a job you do because you enjoy it. It's a job which requires you to develop professional knowledge and skills. And if you want to be a really high performance person, it's a job you have to be proud of. You have to live and breathe it. You have to genuinely enjoy it. You have to strive to keep learning so that you can eventually become an expert in your chosen field. If this sounds like a lot of hot air to you, then I suggest that you should not attempt to build a career in selling. You will be beaten before you begin. A negative attitude towards your work will guarantee one thing — failure.

The essential thing about selling is that it is a people business. It focuses on communication. Today's seller is:

- A good listener rather than a good talker.
- A good questioner who encourages people to talk honestly about their needs and problems.
- Genuinely interested in people.
- Good at gathering information and using it to help people to satisfy their needs and solve their problems.

You should notice that the person I have described above might easily have been a psychiatrist, a solicitor or even a member of the clergy. They're all good listeners and good problem solvers too. In fact, good communication is basic to achieving success in any profession. We all know that the doctor who gets the most business is the one with the best bedside manner, not the person with the first class honours degree who can't stand people . . . and shows it.

This is what more and more business people are realising every day. The skills of the salesperson are very similar to the skills possessed by other professionals, and they are essentially communication skills. That's why the banking industry is now trying to teach its managers sales techniques. Accountants and engineers now realise that people skills are just as important as technical skills. If you can't communicate properly with your clients, they'll go to someone who can.

So remember this basic lesson as you read through this book: selling isn't something you do to people; it's something you do with people, through effective communication and sensitive interaction.

I've spent most of my life in selling. It's a career I'm proud of. And I've learnt a lot about selling . . . often the hard way. But on the basis of that experience, I have developed a description of the processes involved in making a sale which I call *The Sales Cycle*. It consists of a series of labelled steps designed to make selling a cinch. Here they are, together with the chief objective behind each step:

1. Prospect *Objective:* to seek out new business opportunities.

2. Rapport *Objective:* to build the client's confidence in you.

3. Explore *Objective:* to find out what they want.

4. Present *Objective:* to demonstrate that your product/service is the one that they need/want.

5. Handle *Objective:* to identify and remove any road blocks in the way of the sale.

6. Test *Objective:* to establish that communication is really taking place.

7. Close *Objective:* to wrap up the transaction in a way that leaves everyone satisfied . . . especially the client.

8. After-sales service *Objective:* to keep the door open for further business.

So there it is! A list of eight easy-to-follow steps.

In this book I'm going to expand on each step to show you in detail what it means and how it fits into the cycle as a whole. I'm going to show you how to make the sales cycle work for you in your career. But before we get into details you must remember two things:

1. Sales go at different speeds. Some go very slowly, while others go so quickly that you don't really notice that the process has commenced. But believe me, all sales go through the eight steps of the sales cycle. You have to learn to recognise what's happening so that you can use it to your advantage.

2. You will screw things up sometimes. We all do. But when things go wrong, don't panic! Refer to the sales cycle and ask '**What if**'?

'**What**' would I do '**if**' I had to do it again?

What use is that, you say? Well, basically, the sales cycle is a checklist of things that happen before, during and after the sale. It helps you to locate where things went wrong so that you won't do the same thing again. In other words, it helps you to learn from experience. It gives you something constructive to do to plan the future. It helps to put you in control of your own life, and that makes it a really powerful selling tool.

Now, before we start up the sales merry-go-round for your first ride, I should take some time to tell you about three key words to at least ensure a safe step onto the carousel. These magic words can bring you much success or grief. It's up to you. One sure thing is that over the last five years I have worked with thousands of salespeople and the high power performance people are 'doing' the magic words every day. Well, what are the words you say? They start with the letters:

G A O

Years ago it was, 'Here is your desk, here is your phone, your name is ''GO'' so go for it'.

Today your new name is 'GAO', meaning — GET ABSOLUTELY ORGANISED.

Before you start the sales cycle, start with yourself and consider whether you've been on the sales merry-go-round before.

Read this page if you are *new* to selling

If you are new to selling, your first step is *product knowledge*. This builds confidence, so here is an idea that will help you to get into the fast lane.

The idea came to me some years ago when we started a brand new salesperson in our company. I suggested that she keep a list of every question that somebody asked her for the next thirty days, and at the end of each day, find out the answer to that question.

By thirty days, your product knowledge will have increased by 80 per cent. Why? Because for the next thirty days you will get asked the same questions. Sure the people change, their faces and names will be different, but the questions will be the same. We call this technique the:

Q & A Approach to product knowledge

Why not get started on this idea now? Simply grab a piece of plain paper and rule a line down the centre like this:

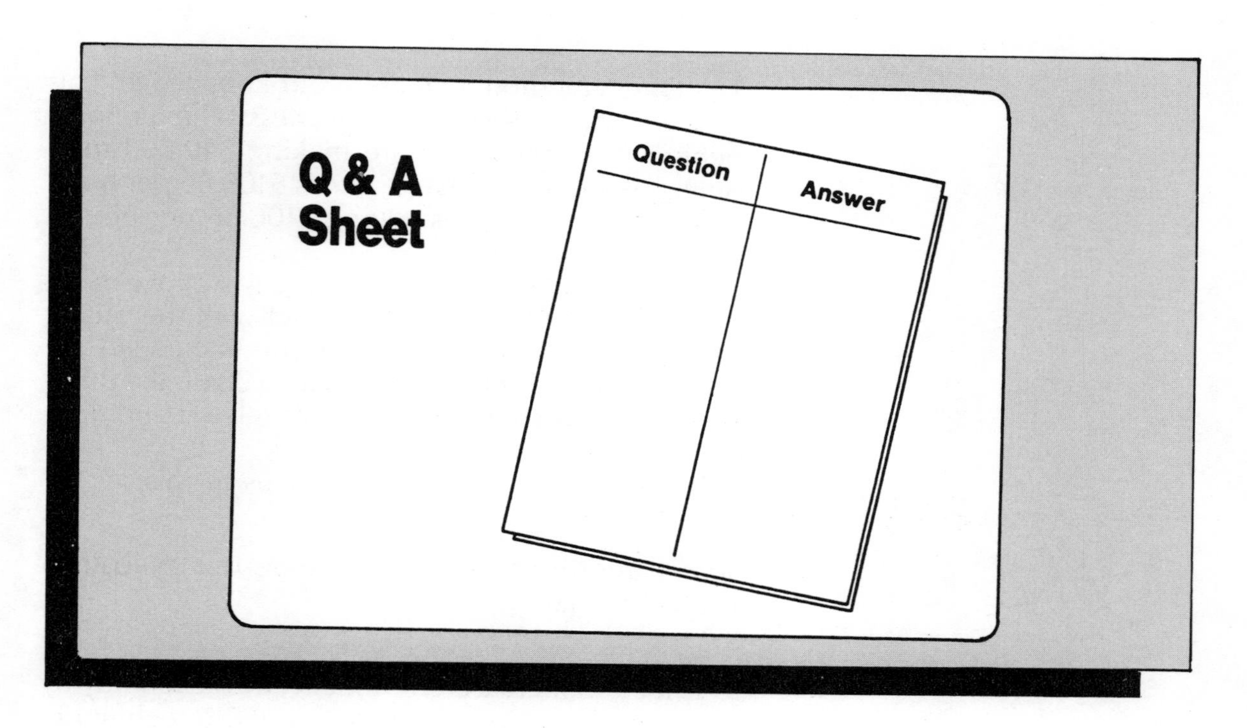

Now here is what you do. Let's say I ask you 'What year did the *Titanic* sink?', or 'Does this computer have 64K of memory?' Instead of saying, 'I don't know', which actually destroys your personal credibility, say 'May I check that for you and get back to you please?'

That then goes in your question column and you find out, record the answer and after thirty days you actually increase your product knowledge by 80 per cent. Review your sheet each week. This approach is simple but very effective. Try it.

Read this page if you are *new,* and read this page if you are *experienced*

The Q & A method increases your knowledge. This idea will increase your *effectiveness*. The rationale behind it is that if you are making $40,000 from selling, your hourly charge rate is $106.66 per hour. Shock, horror! If I was getting $106.66 per hour, I would be a millionaire.

It works like this: they say the only way we make a sale is eyeball to eyeball contact with the buyer. They also say that we are only spending less than 35 per cent of our time eyeball to eyeball, the other 65 per cent is spent in all sorts of related and non-related activities.

So there are two messages for us in this:

1. To sell more we need to increase our eyeball to eyeball contact.

2. We need to increase our effectiveness each day by using the Error Correction Review (ECR) technique.

It's quite simple. At the end of each day take ten minutes to relax and take a deep breath. Open your diary and rule a line across the bottom of the page and sit back, put your feet up, re-run and analyse the day. Say to yourself, 'If I had today over again, how could I have been more effective?' Then prepare your active statement and commit it to paper.

Using this idea, each day is a 'lesson' day. So, if we missed the sale because we were late, the ECR action would show, 'Don't Be Late'. Now show the action for your new plan, then tomorrow learn from yesterday's mistakes.

The ECR technique is straightforward so why not rule up your diary now. From the bottom of the page rule the line for the next month, then start the process each day, it's all part of Getting Absolutely Organised.

Now we have got 'GAO', let's start the sales cycle — with 'Prospect'. It's the first step you can use in the development of a successful and satisfying life as you venture into the world of sales.

1 PROSPECT

Your business is a bit like your garden. It can either blossom or become overrun by weeds, depending on your attitude to nurturing growth. To attract prospects (potential buyers) to your business, or garden, you have to establish it properly. This takes a lot of careful planning and hard work, but it can be very rewarding. When you've finally got it just the way you hoped it would be, you can briefly stand back and look at it with justifiable pride and satisfaction.

But it mustn't stop there. You have to weed and water it. If you don't, growth will be stifled. Once it stops growing it starts to die and your business will never flourish.

You know, of course, that your established clients are the basis on which you build your company. But growth is a sign of health and vigour. If your business isn't growing, there's a good chance that it's in the early stages of decay. Don't let the rot set in. Develop a well-organised attack and seek out new business opportunities, so that your company will prosper and grow. In other words, think about developing an effective approach to prospecting.

In the old days it was believed that there was only one way to look for new business. That was to open the shop, sit back and wait for things to happen. That's a sure way to go broke, isn't it?

If you have a good product or valuable service to sell, it's probable that somewhere in your district, every day, a lot of people will be wanting to buy exactly what you have to sell. Of course, they might buy it from someone else. So what can you do?

You can make sure that they actually *know that you are in the business*.

How can you make sure that those potential buyers turn to you rather than to your opposition?

Well, one thing you can do is to put into operation the following prospecting plan. It won't solve all your problems, but it will give a basis on which you can build your own program for business growth.

1. Work on your communication skills

As I said in the introduction, selling is a people business. You have to like people, and you have to show that you like them.

- Look them in the eye.
- Smile.
- Ask them questions.
- Listen to their answers with real interest.
- Make them feel important.

If you're approachable and helpful, if people feel comfortable with you, then they'll turn to you, rather than the other person, when the time comes to buy.

2. Don't be a shrinking violet

Make sure people know what you do for a living. It's great to be nice, friendly Henry Ford who is in the tennis club, but it's even better to be nice, friendly Henry Ford who's in the tennis club and sells cars.

If people don't know what you do for a living you're not giving them the chance to deal with you or tell others what you do. It would be stupid to try aggressive selling on your social acquaintances. What you do for a living is an important part of you. It inevitably comes up in conversation. One of the first questions people ask is, 'What do you do for a living?'

So don't be shy. If an acquaintance is looking for your product and doesn't contact you, you're obviously doing something wrong. Make sure people know what you have to offer, and be certain that you're the type of person they'll want to deal with.

3. Build your personal network

a) Leave business cards

Okay, it's important to recognise that there is new business to be found amongst your friends and acquaintances. But you can't expect your social contacts to be your only source of business growth. Your network has to reach out into every area of your daily life.

Your hairdresser, your accountant, your mechanic and your grocer can all help you to make sales. Of course, you can't expect them to sell for you, but if you have built friendly relationships with them they'll be pleased to help people to find you.

So help them to help you. Give them a stack of business cards. Then, if anyone asks them where they can find the type of product or service you sell, they just have to offer them one of your attractively designed cards which shows clearly:

- Who you are
- What you sell
- Where to find you.

It's an easy way to reach out into the market to new customers. Be sure you use it.

b) Distribute company gifts

There are all sorts of useful things that people will be pleased to receive as gifts. For example, pens, desk calendars, key rings. They should all have your company name and telephone number embossed on them. Then, when someone asks your hairdresser or your newsagent where they can buy a computer or rent a car, it's easy for them to refer the enquirer on to you. They only have to look at their desk calendar or key ring to find the essential facts.

c) Use letterhead for all your correspondence

What I've just said about business cards and gifts also applies to the writing paper you use. Whenever you write a letter, make sure that it's on attractively designed letterhead. Your company name and address, your own name and a contact telephone number and facsimile number should be clearly displayed at the top of each page. The critical point is that you need to keep your name and your product in the minds of those who might be in a position to refer business to you, and using your letterhead, even for informal notes, is a simple way of doing that.

Remember this! Referrals are the most important source of sales, no matter what you sell. If you show a genuine interest in the people you meet through your personal and business contacts, then they'll want to help you make sales. So make it easy for people to help you by leaving cards, distributing give aways and using letterhead correspondence.

4. Set up a client contact system

People like to be remembered. If you can recall their names and some personal details it will be appreciated. So you should look for techniques which will help you improve your memory.

One simple way to do this is to keep a contact card system. When you meet someone new make a special effort to remember the details of most importance. Listen carefully, then, when you get a chance, record name, spouse's name, number of children and interests on a file card. Other details like address and telephone numbers can be easily added later. If the person concerned becomes a client you can use the card to remind you of the details which will personalise your contact with them. And you should also use the card to record what is said on each occasion you speak to them.

The card system has a number of purposes. It helps you to improve your memory and to maintain cordial contacts with the people in your personal network. But most of all it puts you in command of information which will make you more efficient. A quick glance at a card will remind you of your previous contact with this person so that you know what was said and what happened as a result. Remembering the details creates confidence and trust, and a card system, conscientiously maintained, will ensure that you do remember them.

On the following page is a sample of the card system we use in our workshops. Why not set up your own system today?

CLIENT CONTACT CARD

FILE UNDER

NAME	
ADDRESS	
PHONE HOME	
WORK	
DETAILS	
CONTACTED	

5. Be visible in the marketplace

Even if you have the greatest product in the field, it won't do you any good if buyers don't think of you when they set out to make a purchase. So you have to think of ways of making yourself visible in the marketplace.

The most obvious way to do this is to advertise. Use the local newspapers and radio stations, and don't forget the yellow pages. But there are other ways as well.

Today, sellers are PRO-ACTIVE not REACTIVE — they go out and make the calls. If customers don't know what you're selling they won't think of you when they are looking for the type of product you are offering. You have to be visible and so does your product.

There are three basic types of prospecting calls.

1. Cold calls You don't know them, they don't know you.

2. Warm calls You know them, they don't want you.

3. Hot calls They know you, they trust you and they have a need.

A good friend of mine, Kermit Boston, is Director for Training at McGraw-Hill in New York. In a recent seminar of his that I attended, he noted that it costs $260 to deploy a salesperson just to 'try' a single cold call. So when you are out there, remember that it is costing the company $260 just for you to talk to that prospect.

The next step from cold calling is pre-call planning. Pre-call planning puts you in the classification of warm to hot. Pre-call planning means doing your homework before you call on the prospect. This type of call puts you in control — it's also much more cost effective then just grabbing your black bag and heading off for a few 'drop in and see' calls.

Pre-call planning saves hours on the road. Instead of hitting the road, *hit the research* and find out information on your prospects. Information can come from numerous sources such as:

- The media
- Personal friends or business contacts
- New businesses opening and directories
- Telephone books
- Keeping your eyes and ears open.

Pre-call planning allows you to control your time with a particular prospect.

If used effectively:

1. *You* decide before the call if you want the business.
2. *You* control your time.
3. *You* make the moves to open the account.
4. *You* use persistence to get the account.

There are SEVEN clearly defined steps to pre-call planning that are listed on the next page.

We will briefly discuss the first three steps in this chapter, while the rest of the book will further develop these and the final four steps in more detail.

Pre-Call Planning

1. **Identify the target prospects**

Is this the business you want?

2. **Research *their* position**

Will this be a good account, who are the decision makers?

3. **Make contact**

Set up your appointment.

4. **Build rapport — just open the door**

Don't sell the product, sell yourself.

5. **Explore**

the DBM

Explore the Dominant Buying Motive. What are their needs?

6. **Plan presentation — around the DBM**

Plan your presentation around their needs.

7. **Knock it Over!**

Test your information then close.

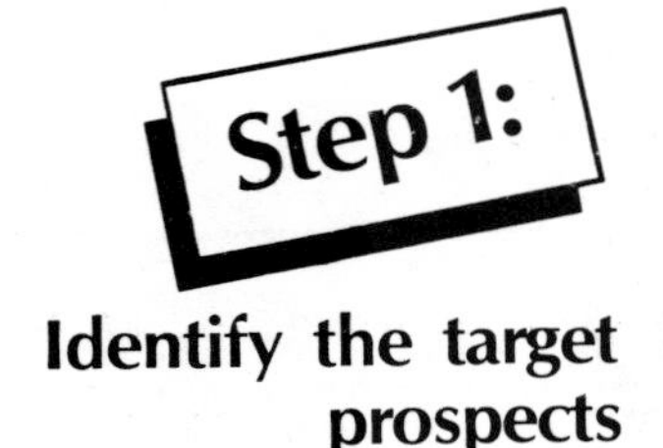

Identify the target prospects

Is there a new company in town that might be interested in what you're selling? Has one of your contacts told you about a potential buyer? Perhaps you've noticed an advertisement for a company that seems a possible client.

There are many ways you can get leads on possible sources of new business. You have to develop the habit of identifying those leads so that you can decide whether they deserve to be followed up. Ask yourself if a prospect is worth chasing. If the answer is yes, then simply move on to the next step.

Research their position

I am constantly amazed by the number of salespeople who call on me without having any idea of what type of business I am engaged in. These people are a source of irritation. They waste my time and their own. Make sure you don't do it.

Before you make a call on any of the companies you have identified as possible customers, do a little research. It's not hard to get a basic idea of any company's purpose and potential needs. You can ask around amongst your contacts. You can telephone the office secretary, or you can make an informal call on the office and speak to the receptionist. When you do this, remember that you are not selling at this stage. You are just making contact and gathering some information about the firm.

Whatever way you do it, make sure you get the information before you make formal contact, not *during* the interview.

Make contact

Once you know something about the company and have an accurate idea about how your product might be of interest, telephone for an appointment.

REMEMBER: YOU ARE STILL NOT SELLING

Make your call. Tell the client who you are and what you do. Ask for ten minutes of her time so that you can explain your product. If you get a negative response, try saying something like this:

> 'Ms Smith, I am not trying to sell you anything. I just want to have the chance to show you a cost-saving method of doing business.'

Make sure you keep the appointment to ten minutes. Demonstrate that you can do what your competitors can't do: give better service, provide better equipment at a lower price and cut costs.

Then leave your brochures and business card and get out. They know who you are now, and what you have to offer. When the next time to purchase comes along you're in with a chance. And that puts you ahead of all the others who haven't bothered to make personal contact with the firm.

Keep in mind that the first call you make should be a door opener call. Of course, if the client wants to place a $10,000 order with you, you won't say,

> 'Doug says I have to walk you through the pre-call planning stages.'

6. Project a positive company image

You might have the best business of its kind in town, but if your premises are messy, your car is always dirty and your office workers are offhand or rude, then you're not likely to have people beating on your door to do business with you.

If you really want to be successful you have to be sure that your company image is at least as good as your product. Here are some points you should check if you want to project a company image which will attract business rather than drive potential clients away at the first point of contact.

a) The first point of contact with your company is often the telephone. You can grab them or lose them right there. When your potential clients ring your office, here is one of the things that can happen: before they can say a word the voice on the other end says, 'Will you hold on for a moment please.' And then they wait — or perhaps they don't. Maybe they decide right then not to bother further with your company.

Make certain that you are careful to ensure that the person who does take calls is given some basic advice about how to make telephone contact with your company as pleasant and productive as possible.

Here are some of the most important things to remember about using the telephone to generate business.

- Remember that you can't be seen. The caller only has your voice to guide them, so make sure that it is friendly and that your manner is helpful. They can't see your dazzling smile, or that you're being asked to do sixty things at the same time. As far as they're concerned their call is the only one you have to handle. In fact, it's the most important call you'll have all day. And that's the way you have to handle it, because it *might* be the most important call you get all day.

- Listen carefully, and without interruption, to what the caller has to say. Always have a notepad and pencil on hand to take down the caller's name and telephone number and to record the details of the enquiry.

- Make sure that the call is concluded to the satisfaction of the caller. Be certain that they have received the information they wanted.

- Secure an appointment. Selling is nearly always done face-to-face. So be certain that you say something like, 'When would it be suitable for you to have our product demonstrated?'

One of the most important qualities you need as a seller is to be approachable. So be sure that your telephone acts as an open doorway to your company, not as a barrier which makes access and information difficult to obtain.

b) When potential clients do get as far as your office, make certain that the premises are clean, attractive and give the impression that the company is businesslike and efficient. Again, personal contacts are important. When the buyer walks through your door, they should get prompt, courteous service. Otherwise they mightn't wait.

c) It isn't just your office that has to look right. The people in your premises have to look reliable and efficient too. That means weird hairstyles and extreme styles of dress have no place in most business offices — unless that's what you happen to be selling. In general, your aim should be to dress and groom yourself in a way that will make your clients feel comfortable. And that means, a safety pin through your left nostril is not a good idea. Dress fashionably, but don't scare the customers away.

d) If you have a fleet of company cars it has to be understood that the car is a mobile extension of the company. The cars don't need to be BMWs, but they should be recent models. They should look as if they are owned by a prosperous, successful company. And they should be clean and odour-free. Sales representatives are entitled to smoke but they don't have the right to lose customers because they forget to empty the ashtrays regularly. If you want your company to look good in the marketplace, your cars have to look good too.

7. Guard your reputation

Advertising is an essential aspect of ensuring the growth of your company. But the best advertisement you can have is a satisfied customer.

Too many people stop trying when the sale is made. This is really stupid. It's what happens after the sale that builds your reputation.

Getting the lowest possible premium on an insurance policy might make you feel good for a while, but if the company is difficult about paying claims, or if they take six months to send a cheque, then you'll wish that you'd gone elsewhere. Or if you find that the bargain you got on your new microcomputer means that you have to assemble it yourself, and that you have to send it to Tokyo for repairs, then you might decide that it wasn't a bargain at all.

If you really care about your clients, and give them the type of service you'd like yourself, then your reputation will grow and so will your sales. A basic maxim of selling is 'NO TRUST/NO SALE', and trust develops out of honest, efficient service before and after the sale. DON'T FORGET IT!

8. Establish a 'new business whiteboard'

An important part of developing an effective prospecting program is to stay aware of the possibilities, and to keep easily accessible records of the stage you have reached in your contacts with the people you have identified as potential buyers.

Head off to your local business supplies firm and buy a large whiteboard. Put it up in an obvious place in your office and call it the *New Business Whiteboard*. Keep it as a visual record of new and possible sources of business. It can hold press cuttings, business cards, brochures you have collected, and anything that is a guide to a possible sale. It's a stimulus to action, but it isn't action, so be sure that you also create an action column so that each day you can do your pre-call planning around your new business whiteboard.

It's true that you could keep the same information in a notebook, but the whiteboard puts the information up where it can't be ignored. If it's impossible to avoid seeing the things you should be doing, it's much harder to avoid or forget this very important aspect of promoting sales. DO IT!

Now, before we sum up this chapter, I'd like to pay special attention to a key part of prospecting. It is a technique that helps the salesperson to save on the ever-increasing cost of travelling around trying to 'drum up' prospects.

Nowadays, apart from saving money, everybody is talking about reducing heart disease, and the way to do this is to walk more, eat less and be aware. So, what has a healthy heart got to do with selling, I hear you ask? Simply this: ten years ago we were telling you to walk your legs off and to make a lot of calls on prospects. However, times have changed.

We know that it costs a company $260 just to put a salesperson on the street to make a cold call. This being the case, how can we make the walk more cost effective?

The experts call it *telemarketing*. It's letting your fingers do the walking. With this in mind, I interviewed Martin Farrugia, a telemarketer with the AMP Society. He believes that by the twenty-first century, 60 to 70 per cent of all products and services will be dealt with by telephone.

Like many other business and sales activities, most people don't approach telemarketing with a definite plan. At the end of our discussion, I put together a simple six step guide called the 'Six Ways to Build or Muscle Up a Successful Telephone Prospecting Technique'. I like to think of it in terms of a body builder warming up for and participating in a Mr Universe competition, because it takes a lot of practice, sweat, tears and rejection to get your telemarketing technique right.

Sizing up

Be aware that prospecting is a numbers game. There will only be a small percentage that you are successful with in getting to the next round. But we have to make the calls to get the business. Estimate how many calls you intend to make to predetermine your number of appointments. We have found that if you make twenty calls, you can expect to set up two qualified appointments if your telephone technique is up to scratch.

Prepare to flex

Set up a telephone script that you are comfortable with in the same way that a body builder has a set routine. The prospect needs to know three things that you must have a standard answer for:

- Who you are
- Why you are calling
- What you can do for them.

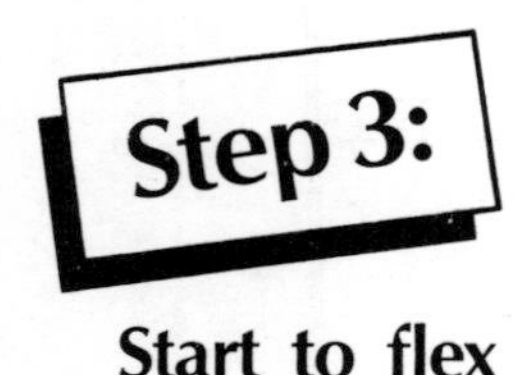

Start to flex

If the script is in black and white in front of you, you can develop a consistent, successful approach as you become more experienced. Don't be afraid to try new questions (poses) to impress the prospect and improve your overall routine.

Hold the spotlight

Stay on track, don't let your prospect drift all around the place. Remember you are on centre stage, so stay there. Be absolutely courteous and polite and use their name constantly.

Titillate the audience

Concentrate on selling yourself on the telephone. Build up trust and warm the listener to you. Handle objections without too much emotion or drama and maintain a strong but calm act of communication. Be prepared to listen.

Win through to the next round

Sell the appointment not the product or service. Telephones are goldmines if we dig in the right places. Even Mr Universe had to work through a number of elimination tournaments and rounds to get to the final. You will have to make a lot of telephone calls before winning through to an appointment round.

Here is a chart that Martin uses on his prospect calls:

Weekly Telemarketing Chart

PHONE CALLS MADE	
TOTAL	
PERSON REACHED	
TOTAL	
APPOINTMENTS MADE	
TOTAL	

SUMMARY FOR WEEK
CALLS MADE ______
PEOPLE REACHED ______
APPOINTMENTS MADE ______

Using the correct technique requires a great deal of practice and patience. Like Mr Universe building muscles and tone, your telemarketing technique must be built-up, and fine-tuned over time.

Summing up

Growth in sales is essential. If your business isn't growing then it's probably dying. Develop a positive program to seek out and generate new business opportunities. Pursue an effective telemarketing technique to develop new prospects.

If your product or service is a good one the problem isn't that buyers don't exist. It is a matter of making sure that when the time to buy comes, prospects include you in the people they turn to.

Much of your business will come from referrals so you have to maximise the number of referrals to your company. Use your personal network so that as many people as possible know who you are, what you sell and where to find you.

Adopt the pre-call planning technique I've described, to save you time and money. Do your homework and put yourself in control right at the start of the sales cycle.

Some clients will just want to walk in and make a purchase. Be as visible as possible so that your business is the one they walk into. This means advertising. It means working on your company image. It also means building a reputation for reliability and efficiency, and making sure that you give the best possible after-sales service.

You can't sit back and wait for the sales to roll in, even if your reputation is impeccable and you have made yourself visible and accessible in the market-place. You have to go out into the business world to make people aware of you and your product. Start a new business whiteboard.

Carefully identify selling possibilities, and then engage in pre-call planning and low-key awareness, making appointments with the people who make the decisions about what is to be bought.

If you are personally known to the client, your chances of making the sale are greater. If your previous contact has left a favourable impression, your chances are even better. If you are known and trusted in the broader marketplace, you are really in there with a great chance of actually making the sale. The idea is to stop them ever getting as far as the yellow pages. Don't let their fingers do the walking.

To simplify things keep in mind this 3A guide to business growth.

1. Awareness: The potential buyer has to know who you are and what you sell.

2. Accessibility: You have to be easy to find and easy to deal with. Some people are easy to find and hard to do business with.

3. Approval: The approval of the individual buyer and the business community at large is the surest basis for continued growth. A good reputation is your most valuable business asset.

Your business is like a garden. You have to keep working on it to make it grow. But sheer hard work is not enough. Good planning is essential if it's going to be really successful. This chapter has given you a plan. Follow it, or something similar, and it shouldn't be too long before you see your business blossom.

2 BUILDING RAPPORT... THE BIG STEP

Think about some time in your life when you felt really uncomfortable. It's different for everyone but it might have been something like this. You are at a wedding reception and you've been placed next to someone you haven't seen for years. You try to start a conversation. You ask about his business. He says he was declared bankrupt last month. So you change direction. You lean across and speak to the woman next to him and say something like, 'It must be at least five years since I last saw you Debbie. I suppose all the kids are at school by now.' He says that this isn't Debbie. They were divorced three years ago and she's refusing access to the children. You resort to the weather. That's always safe. 'Lovely fine weather we've had this year.' He tells you that after Debbie left him he sold his printery and tried growing avocados. It was the drought that sent him bankrupt. The bloke who bought his business just made his first million.

Can you remember an occasion something like that? Okay. Focus on it for a minute. Try to capture the feeling of discomfort again; the desperate realisation that you didn't know what to say or do next. Remember the feeling that all you wanted to do was to escape from the situation as quickly as possible and never return again. You know what that feeling is? That's zero rapport. And it's something salespeople have to avoid like the plague.

Now, I might have exaggerated a little bit in my example but it isn't hard to get yourself into situations like that, especially when you're trying to establish a comfortable relationship with people you hardly know. Nearly every potential buyer will be a stranger to you. But you won't make many sales if you treat them like a stranger. It's very important to make them feel at ease with you, because it's only when they feel that sense of ease and trust that you can be fairly sure of making the sale. And that's what rapport is, an atmosphere of relaxation and trust between people that makes conversation easy, and allows questions to be asked and answered without awkwardness or embarrassment. As we shall see, this requires a great deal of versatility on your behalf.

Of course, different people talk about rapport-building in different ways. These days some experts talk about the 'tension/trust theory' (that's much the same thing as rapport). They say that whenever we meet someone new there is inevitably a certain amount of tension in the situation. We have no real basis for communication. We don't know anything about them or the lives they live. There is no common body of experience to share or refer to. But it's totally different when we are with old friends because there has been a great deal of trust built between the people involved, trust that has developed during years of friendship.

Trust reduces tension in social situations and it is

based on the things we share with other people. It makes communication easier and allows our social contacts to be pleasant and rewarding. With new acquaintances it takes time to build the common links which are the basis for friendship. But we always try to get them started. Most of us when we meet someone new try to establish a basis for friendly future contacts. We don't assume that it's just going to be too difficult and that, anyway, we'll probably never meet them again. We try to open up possible topics of conversation. We probe for points of contact in our lives. You know how it goes. 'I see from your badge that you're in Apex. I'm Doug Malouf from the Wollongong Club.' or 'I went to Central Heights High too. When were you there?'

This search for common links is a way of setting the basis for communication. Without a body of shared experience it is almost impossible to talk to someone else. At the beginning it needn't be a shared experience. All that is required is that both parties know about the same types of things. They know what it's like to be in a Rotary club, or to have gone to a specific school. As a result, initial links are enriched by a knowledge of things which have been done together and which form a much more comfortable and enjoyable basis for communication. A friendship is usually born.

Establishing a productive and pleasant relationship with your clients is important. It is essentially the same type of process involved in meeting new people in your social life. Although it might not be desirable to try to make personal friends of all your clients, it is still true that your business will prosper if you and your clients go on to develop a solid basis of mutually satisfying contacts. This will ensure that your communication with them is smooth and cordial. The truly successful salesperson is the one whose clients keep coming back, year after year.

Making first impressions count

So far I've been talking about building rapport in a general sense. I've drawn my examples from the development of social contacts, and related it to the way we try to establish social relationships and build friendships. That's fine. One of the first lessons you need to learn about selling is that the way you behave as a salesperson is essentially no different to the way good communicators behave in any situation.

Of course there are some differences between casual social contacts and the types of contacts you have to establish with potential buyers. In your social life you can afford not to worry if you antagonise someone. You don't lose sleep if you fail to establish a close friendship with every new acquaintance. And you don't have to be told that friendships sometimes develop slowly. It's not uncommon to develop a close relationship with someone who didn't appeal to you much at first. As you meet them over and over again, you have the chance to modify your first impressions.

It's not usually like that in the world of business. First impressions are much more important. There's a good chance that a poor first impression is the only impression a potential buyer will form, because they'll walk away from you and you'll never see them again. In the world of selling, the first stage in successful rapport-building has to be done quickly. You have to make people feel at ease with you as soon as possible. It has been established that more sales are lost in the first three minutes of contact than at any other time during the whole selling process. You have to be able to make your clients feel relaxed and comfortable as quickly as possible. If you make them feel awkward or foolish, or if you antagonise them in those first few minutes, you can forget it. You'd better move on to the next prospect.

So, how can you make first impressions count as much as possible?

1. Check your appearance

In most cases you'll be seen first, before you open your mouth. Make sure that the way you look makes a favourable impression.

a) Grooming

Make sure that your hair is neat and conservatively styled at all times. Be sure your clothing is recently cleaned and well pressed. If your grooming suggests that you don't take trouble over these personal details, it won't be surprising if potential clients suspect that you might not take any trouble over their problems either.

b) Dress

For most salespeople the golden rule of dressing well is to avoid extremes. A skirt, thongs and an 'Iron Maiden' tee-shirt are nice . . . but not if you're selling office equipment. On the other hand, you won't be doing much for your image if you borrow your grandfather's three piece, double-breasted, blue pin-striped serge suit either . . . You know, the one he's been wearing to funerals for the last forty years.

The way you dress does create a powerful impression. It can suggest that you are modern, efficient, reliable and trustworthy. Or . . . it can suggest that you're a disorganised, sloppy, out-of-date sharp dealer. The choice is yours. It's one aspect of your public self that really is completely under your own control.

Remember that building rapport means making people feel comfortable in your company. So dress fashionably. Choose clothes and hairstyles that are modern, but which are on the conservative side of the fashion spectrum. Most people have a fairly clear idea of what a respectable, honest and competent businessperson looks like. So please take my advice . . . Don't surprise them!!

c) Smile

There isn't much I can add to this. A genuine, friendly smile will do more to break the ice than anything else. And you'll find it easy to smile if you like people and you like selling. If you don't possess these two qualifications, you should think of doing something else with your life.

2. Check your communication skills

No matter how good you look you can still self-destruct instantly if your communication skills are poor. The first words you speak to a new client will be particularly important. If they make you sound nasty, stupid or dishonest, that's the way you'll be remembered. So here are a few tips about how to make those first words count.

The common courtesy pack

As you read these tips, they may seem simple and logical to you. If so, that's great! Don't forget them. Unfortunately, from what I've seen in recent years, such basic communication courtesies appear to be lacking in too many of today's salespeople.

a) Speak first

Take the initiative. Open up the lines of communication. That doesn't mean that you should grab their hands or pat them on the back. If you do that they're likely to start feeling for their wallets. But a friendly, pleasant acknowledgment of their presence is basic to the development of a good relationship with a potential buyer.

b) Speak slowly

This might seem to be a trivial point but it's really very important. If you speak too quickly, people will have trouble understanding you. They'll smile and nod while you talk to them. Then, as you walk away wondering why those friendly people didn't respond to your offers of help, they'll be looking at one another and saying, 'What the hell was that all about?' And the sad thing is that you'll probably never know that you've failed as a communicator, or what you can do to avoid the same mistake again.

So make a deliberate attempt to slow your speech and see if it makes a difference.

c) Ask questions

All the great communicators will tell you that it isn't how much you say, or even what you say that makes you a good conversationalist, it's the questions you ask. Don't try to be clever or amusing. If people want to be entertained they'll go to the theatre.

And you don't even have to get straight down to business either. What you have to do first is bridge the gap between you. A good way to do that is by asking questions that are designed to draw answers and establish contact between you and this stranger who might trust you to sell them something. It isn't possible to suggest specific approaches because what you say will depend on the people and the situation, but let's try a couple of scenes.

You've been admitted to the office of the sales manager who has a photograph of her children on her desk. You might say something like, 'I see you have a family. How old are your children?' Or, you approach a man on your showroom floor who is wearing the badge of a football club on his coat collar. So you say something like, 'I see that you're involved with the Bears. How do you think they'll go next year?'

All right. What's so great about that? Nothing really. But notice a couple of things about those scenes:

(i) The questions are based on careful observation. Look closely at your clients, or look around the outer office to try to pick up anything that might help you to establish contact.

(ii) The comments and questions aren't too personal. It is wise to avoid being personal too early.

Think of questions that invite people to talk to you

in a pleasant, easy way. You should note that our examples above can't just be answered with a simple 'Yes' or 'No'. They are related to topics which are likely to be of interest to the person concerned.

I'm not suggesting that you try to engage in long personal conversations with new customers. They are interested in buying and you are interested in selling, and both of you know that. But human communication is a funny thing. If you just bounce straight up to potential buyers and ask, 'Can I help you?' then you are likely to be fobbed off with something like, 'Not at the moment, thank you. I'll call you if I need assistance.'

If you take a moment to give those people the feeling that you might be interested in them, even if they weren't going to buy anything from you, then you've done something significant. You've acknowledged them. You've made them feel important, and that won't do your chances of making a sale any harm. Believe me!

d) Learn to listen

Asking questions is the way to get people talking, but it won't work if you don't listen with obvious interest to what is said in answer to your questions. Just think of your own experience: if you are talking to someone who is obviously not paying close attention to what you are saying, you feel annoyed or even angry. Failing to pay attention to what someone is saying tells the speaker that they are boring or unimportant.

On the other hand, if someone listens with close attention and obvious interest when we are speaking to them, we feel pleased and flattered. They are telling us that we are someone of significance with interesting things to say. We feel comfortable with these people, we seek out their company, our rapport with them is good.

Good listening involves two basic behaviours:

(i) Looking at the speaker the whole time they are speaking.

(ii) Providing feedback. In other words: smile, nod and ask more questions based on what has already been said.

e) Be positive

It's very important to project yourself as a positive, optimistic person. We all have problems, but the truth is that most people don't want to hear about them. If you spend a lot of time making negative comments, you'll end up talking to yourself.

You can only be positive if you think in positive terms. You have to develop optimistic ways of viewing the world. Most of us have read A.B. Facey's life story, or seen it dramatised on television. I'm sure we have all wondered how he could have called the story of life filled with hardship and sorrows *A Fortunate Life*, but that's the way he saw it. He learned to look at life positively, to value what was good, and not to grieve constantly over misfortune. If you can develop those same mental habits you won't need to worry about how you can project a positive impression of yourself, you'll do it without thinking.

If you still feel you might have problems with being positive, try asking yourself, 'Am I a constant complainer, or am I a constant complimenter?' Looking for things in other people which are worthy of a compliment will start you on the right path to positive thinking and the projection of a positive impression of yourself in your daily communication with friends and clients.

So . . . to become a better communicator, speak less, listen more, be positive and ask questions that give people opportunities to talk about themselves.

The RBT technique – rapport building

Lyn Sellers, International Sales Trainer, travels the world teaching salespeople techniques to build rapport with the customer. She has developed her own method called the 'EVALUATION OF SELLING'. In this program she shows us how selling has moved from the snake-oil salesman approach to the development of customer contact skills. Building rapport is number one.

There is more to building rapport than just the common courtesy pack: we need to go a little deeper than this. But let us have a quick drink first.

Now, when we go out and have a few drinks most of us become a little more animated. But if we know we are driving there is always a little control mechanism keeping us in check — the RBT (Random Breath Test).

The key to my RBT (Rapport-Building Technique) is to recognise that there are also signals, control mechanisms that crop up in conversation with a prospect, which indicate what communication style and steps to take.

I said earlier that it is important to observe your potential clients closely so that we can get some idea of how we might be able to make them feel comfortable. The idea was that we should take note of personal details that might give us clues to mutual topics of conversation. But there are other things we need to observe as well.

Communication is a two-way process. We don't just talk so that we can hear the words. We talk to other people and we respond to the things they communicate to us, and not all of those things are communicated in speech.

A gesture can mean as much as a five-minute speech. A facial expression can stop us in our tracks.

A failure to speak at all can sometimes say far more than the most eloquent speech.

Psychologists have been interested for some time in the different ways people respond to each other. It is suggested that by careful study we can predict or classify the communication style of most people based on their responses. Some call it a response line, but I like to call it the *reaction* line, because it is an individual's *actions* to another that identify them. Some people are highly reactive (pro-active). Others are hardly reactive at all. This can be drawn graphically as shown below.

0 . . . . 50% 100%

LOW . . . . HIGH
REACTOR   REACTOR
(Pro-active)
(Are they DEAD?)   (Will they talk themselves to death?)

How do you rate yourself? Probably, like most of us, you'd say you were somewhere in the middle. Don't worry, there is no right or wrong reaction type. We are all individuals which makes this world the interesting and exciting place that it is.

What is of importance is that according to psychologists, we can fluctuate between the extremes. We can vary our style or reaction to others according to the situation we are in.

For example, if we've been pulled over by the Highway Patrol we'll almost certainly be at the low reaction end of the line in our behaviour. If we're not acting like we're dead, we're explaining that someone else may well be, and that is why we were in such a hurry. If we use very assertive gestures and provide too much feedback we are likely to find ourselves talking to a magistrate instead. But if we are at a party and want to impress someone special, we hit the high reaction end of the line. We're on show! Eye contact is intense, feedback is fierce. You really need to be there to appreciate the animation.

Everyone has a primary reaction type, but we can easily shift gear. We have a range of reaction styles and we can be versatile in the way we use them. Just to prove my point, I'm sure that you're all familiar with the teenager who barely responds to his parents but becomes an animated and active communicator when talking to girls on the beach. Now, this is where the correct use of the Rapport-Building Technique becomes beneficial. Don't blow in the bag just yet. We need to carefully watch the prospective buyer and make an assessment of their reaction style. Then, when you approach them, you needn't make foolish blunders which might destroy any chance you have of establishing a comfortable relationship. Be prepared to change gear to suit the person and the situation.

1. Straighten your attire

You notice that the person on the showroom floor is very low-key in their conversation with a friend. They hardly use any gestures and are speaking in a quiet way with little animation. They're low reactors, so don't come on too strongly, otherwise they'll sum you up as aggressive and will avoid dealing with you. Be careful with the small talk and just get to the point.

2. Maximise eye contact

You are shown into the office of the salesperson. You've seen her joking with the receptionist as she passed through the outer office. She is lively and extroverted. Her voice is self-assured and she uses gestures extensively. She has a pro-active style (high reactor). What does this tell you? You'd better make strong eye contact, listen carefully, show your interest and understanding in your feedback responses, and project yourself confidently or she's likely to write you off as a wimp.

The above two examples are the extremes of the reaction line. In between you will meet all sorts of personality and communication styles. Here's a few more to add to the pack.

3. Talk hand in hand

Very often you'll meet prospects who wave their hands so much when talking that if you tied them behind their backs they couldn't say a thing. How should you react to such 'hand talkers'? Copy them. Use your hands to dramatise your talk. It establishes a sense of affinity. We can take this a step further and suggest that if they fidget, you should fidget too — but that's another story.

4. Match their energy levels

If the prospect is a low-energy person and you speak with a lot of energy, chances are you'll wear them out. They'll walk away thinking they've fought fifteen rounds with Mike Tyson, and you won't sell them anything. Try to match your expressed energy level to the prospect by altering your own.

5. Maintain word pace

As with energy levels for maximum communication impact, it is important to mimic the prospect's word pace. If they're speaking as fast as Speedy Gonzales runs, quicken up your word pace. If they like to speak slowly and calmly, don't overawe them.

Unfortunately, we all tend to judge people in terms of the type of person we believe ourselves to be. But if you want to build rapport quickly with people, you have to be able to match your style to the reaction type of the prospect. Let them see a modified image of themselves because the image in the mirror usually warms our hearts and excites our admiration. That doesn't mean you have to be insincere. As I pointed out before, we all change gears constantly in the way we react to people.

In the commercial world, we don't have much time. If we can't establish cordial contact with people quickly, then we're not likely to succeed in selling them anything. The effective use of the RBT is all about versatility. You must be completely *versatile* in your communication skill and style and adapt yourself accordingly to be 'on par' with the prospects. Remember dinosaurs were poor adaptors and look what happened to them. Don't let it happen to you.

Summing up

A major problem in the selling situation can be lack of trust. Buyers often expect salespeople to mislead them. They think, 'What's the point of asking questions? They wouldn't tell me if there was anything wrong with the product anyway. I'm better just to work it out for myself.'

Now that's silly. The sales representative should be an expert on the product. They should be the best person to provide accurate information. But before they can do the job of helping people to make a decision about whether this product is the best one to suit their needs, we have to overcome the reservations many people have about professional sellers.

Part of the problem is, of course, that we all feel a bit awkward when we are dealing with strangers. So I have suggested that you think about how you do that in your social life, and apply the same principles to your business dealings. You must not approach the potential buyer as someone who might buy something from you. It's vital that you first acknowledge them as individuals, people who have lives and interests of their own that you might like to talk about if you met them at a party. It's your attitude that's important. Remember the common courtesy pack.

I emphasise again that I don't mean that you should actually try to establish close contact with them. Too much small talk, and anything really personal, is likely to send them running for cover. But you have to make sure that the buyer recognises that you, too, are basically a well-intentioned person who is interested in helping them with the problems they are having in making a decision to buy something. If they see you first as a person they can trust, then they will ask you questions and believe your answers, and you are likely to have acquired a client who will return to you, or refer other people to you, even if they don't buy your product this time.

Remember, too, that selling isn't something divorced from the rest of your life. In every conversational situation, in business or pleasure, there is a potential disaster. Even if you look fine, and you are really trying hard to be helpful and discreet, you can destroy contact if you aren't careful enough about what you say and how you say it. So develop your observation skills. Look closely at the situation and the person and think about what you intend to say before you say it. Keep in mind the Rapport-Building Technique and match your reaction patterns to theirs. Remember that if you start badly, it's generally downhill from then on.

Building trust, and establishing a comfortable atmosphere in which it is possible to ask questions is what I mean by establishing rapport. The real problem is that in the world of selling you have to do it quickly. That's why I have emphasised the importance of forming a good first impression. The judgments the buyer makes about you in the first few minutes are the ones that they'll stick to. Remember that you are a stranger to them in those first moments, and most of us distrust strangers, especially strangers who clearly want to sell us something. So check your professional image. Reflect on your communication skills and develop a positive attitude to life and the people around you. MAKE SURE THAT THOSE FIRST THREE MINUTES NEVER COST YOU A SALE.

A positive fact: 'IN THE FIRST THREE MINUTES OF THE SALES PROCESS YOU AND I ARE EITHER SELLING OR SINKING.'

3 EXPLORE

We've established that selling is a two-way communication process. We understand that it's important to ask the right questions, and we are convinced that listening is the most important communication skill of all. We've also discussed ways of keeping the information flowing when we are interviewing clients.

But what you really want to know is how you can improve your sales record, right? Well, that's really what I've been talking about all the time. The good seller asks the right questions and listens efficiently. That's how they can distinguish genuine buyers from the voyeurs, the ones who just enjoy looking. That's how they can show them products that they *know* will be of interest to them and how they are able to maximise the amount of time they spend with people who are likely to make the decision to buy.

You know the old saying, 'You can take a horse to water but you can't force it to drink'. The good salesperson knows how to handle that. First, they make sure that the horse is genuinely thirsty. Then they establish that it is water that the horse wants to drink. Finally, they make sure that the horse has access to water displayed to its best advantage. Under those circumstances even the most stubborn horse is likely to take a drink. And that's how you boost sales! It's based on having the right information about the buyer. And that comes from ASKING THE RIGHT QUESTIONS.

The first time I fully appreciated how important it is to ask the right questions was during a visit to the United States of America. I had developed a sore throat so I went to a local doctor. When my name was called I expected to be shown in to see the doctor, but no! I found myself being interviewed by a nurse instead. He sat with his pen poised and a checklist in front of him. We played twenty questions.

'Have you ever suffered from fallen arches or ingrown toenails?' Good God! He wasn't even at the right end of me! 'Haemorrhoids?' Well at least we were going in the right direction.

He left no stone unturned. We covered every part of my body. Every ache I'd ever had, every pain I'd ever suffered. It took fifteen minutes.

My consultation with the doctor took ten. Armed with the information her nurse had given her about me, she got straight to the cause of my difficulty and took the appropriate steps to cure me.

That got me thinking. I asked myself, 'What actually happened during my visit to the doctor?' It seemed that I had gone through a series of steps.

Firstly, I'd become conscious of a problem so I'd gone to the appropriate person to help me solve it: the doctor.

Then I'd gone through a preliminary interview which gave the doctor a background of essential information about me. Some of the questions seemed a bit strange to me, but they helped the doctor to focus on the real nature of my problem and possible ways of solving it.

Next, the doctor gathered more information from me. She examined me, and asked more specific questions.

Finally, she considered possible solutions to the problem, chose the most appropriate area and took action to cure me.

Looked at in this way it becomes clear that the doctor is essentially a problem solver. And that's what sellers are too. Problem solvers! People come to you because they have a problem and they hope you will be able to help them with it.

The preliminary interview was an important part of the problem-solving process for the doctor. It was an efficient way of gathering information that helped her to do her job more effectively. It permitted the doctor to spend more time doing what she was paid for: curing patients.

That's what a carefully prepared preliminary interview can do for you too. It can help you to spend more time doing what you're paid to do: selling. It can also help you to clarify the nature of your clients' needs, to find the right solutions to their problems and it can make you more efficient and effective.

When I got home I sat down to think about the types of questions a seller might need to ask during a preliminary interview with a new client. To do that properly I had to think about what was involved in effective selling. What did the seller need to know in order to maximise the chances of making a sale?

I developed what I call the CRAPP formula. This provided me with a simple guide to answering the above question that I could utilise time and time again.

1. 'C' for Capacity

The most successful sellers are the people who spend a high proportion of their time with clients who are both *genuinely interested* in making a purchase, and who are *able* to make the decision to buy.

That means you have to ask questions that help you to:

a) Distinguish genuine buyers from people who are playing games.

b) Discover whether the people you are talking to have the authority to make decisions about purchases. You have to ask yourself: 'Does this person have the CAPACITY to make a purchase?'

2. 'R' for Reasons

It is essential that you discover as quickly as possible what I call the DBMs: your client's Dominant Buying Motive.

In other words, you need to know what made the prospect think they might need *your* product to satisfy their needs or solve their problems. You have to ask yourself: 'What is this person's REASON for buying?'

3. 'A' for Anticipation

Once you know *what* they need, and *why* they need it, you have to know what they *expect* your product to do for them. Let me give you an example. A couple comes into your showroom. They can't fit the family into their car anymore. They *need* a vehicle that holds two adults and five children. But they also *expect* to be able to get 15 kilometres per litre fuel economy. You need to know that before you can talk sensibly to them about the options which are available. You have to ask yourself: 'What does this couple ANTICIPATE that they will get from this purchase?'

4. 'P' for Price

You have to know approximately what your client is able to pay for the purchase.

If you don't have any information about your customer's budget you can destroy all chance of making a sale. There's no better way to demoralise your client than by showing them all the good things their money *can't* buy. Make sure the options you present are within the prospect's means. Ask yourself: 'What PRICE is this person able to pay?'

5. 'P' for Priorities

Finally, you have to know how important the purchase is to your client. Do they feel a pressing need to buy, or are they quite prepared to defer the purchase if conditions aren't quite to their liking?

If they can't get the trade-in price they want, are they prepared to wait for six months? If they can't afford all the features they hoped for, will the prospect use their present equipment for another year? You need to know this to make a judgment about how much time to spend on that client. Ask yourself: 'What are this person's purchasing PRIORITIES?'

So there you have it. How to be the best explorer in town using the CRAPP detector formula.

C. Capacity
R. Reason
A. Anticipation
P. Price
P. Priorities

Feel free to check this 'formula'. Call a friend who is in sales. Ask them what five 'need to knows' they seek to find out about a prospect upon their first meeting.

You'll find a recurring theme of five basic concerns that closely follow the CRAPP formula, no matter what industry or business you are in.

To prove the point, I called upon a few sales professionals I know, and these were their responses:

1. Paul Plumber, who is a totally committed insurance salesman, lists his five 'need to knows' as:
(a) Their age and type of lifestyle.
(b) What is their current financial situation?
(c) Do they have life or insurance policies?
(d) What are their expectations of insurance?
(e) Who will decide upon taking out insurance or not?

Paul also noted that if the interview starts to get too personal, he always stops and politely asks for permission to proceed.

2. Charlie Gall, who has sold more cars than he cares to remember, makes the point not to push the interview process too hard. He focuses on the following 'top five' details:
(a) What style of car they like?
(b) What size car interests them?
(c) What expectations about performance they hold?
(d) Who will make the decision to buy?
(e) When can the rubber hit the road?

3. As a final example, Marie Davis, a real estate agent, sets herself a five point checklist:

(a) What are the true interests of the client?
(b) What is the customer's reason for wanting to buy a house?
(c) What special expectations does the buyer have?
(d) What can the customer afford to pay?
(e) How urgently does the client need the house?

As you can see from these examples, no matter what selling industry you're in, there is a general theme of five key questions/'need to knows' that keep recurring. The exact questions to be asked vary depending on the type of product to be sold.

As a short practice exercise, you may want to try matching the above responses to the CRAPP formula. It's not always a perfect fit, but the principles of conducting a preliminary interview structured around the CRAPP framework are an essential basis for effective selling.

After you've sorted out the CRAPP, put it all together on a simple 15 x 10 cm prospect card.

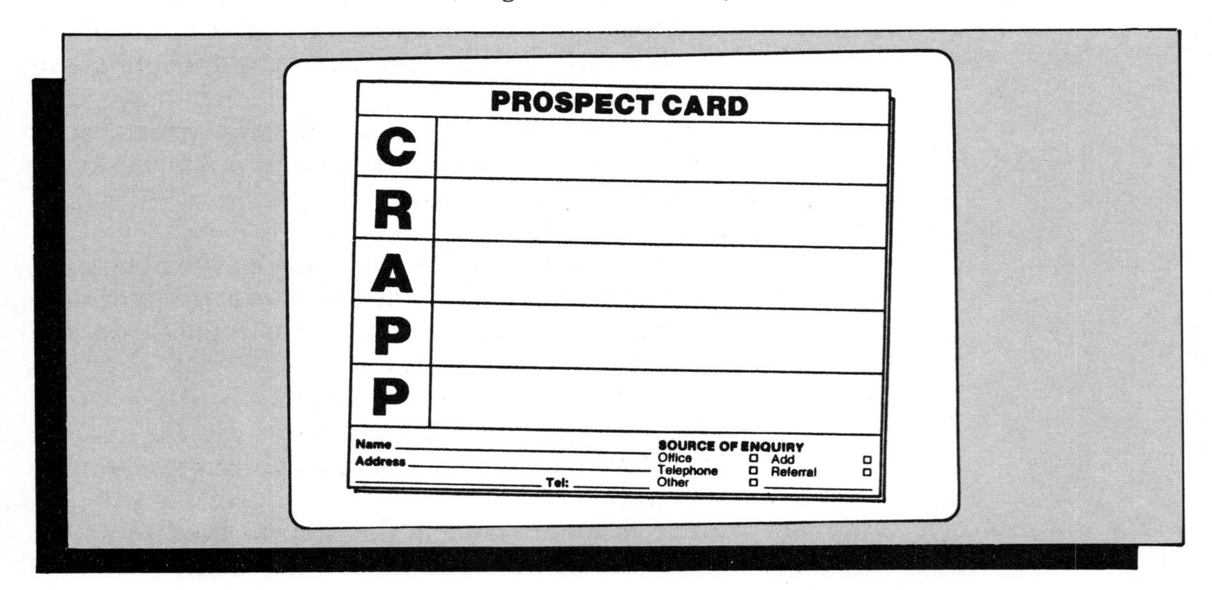
PROSPECT CARD

C	
R	
A	
P	
P	

Name ____________________
Address ____________________
____________ Tel: __________

SOURCE OF ENQUIRY
Office ☐ Add ☐
Telephone ☐ Referral ☐
Other ☐ ____________

Write the person's name, address and contact number, then record the DBM for your memory.

When to write a prospect card depends on the product you are selling. However, whether it's a newspaper advertisement sale for $50 or a computer system for $300,000, a prospect card should be recorded as soon as possible after contact with a prospect has been made.

The next step is to grade the client using this method.

A. Buyer is hot
B. Buyer is warm
C. Buyer is cold
D. Buyer is dead

Then it is all there in black and white to prompt you to follow up the As and Bs and help them make a decision.

Now, we are not very good at follow-up are we? Why is this? It could be fear of rejection: we don't follow-up just in case we get a 'No'. That would be awful. Well, no follow-up — no sales. Why waste the 'Exploring Phase' if we don't intend to follow-up. My friend Jack Cashmore of Illawarra Business Equipment knows the value of follow-up. Years ago when he was building up his clientele he decided he wanted our business. Jack had done his pre-call planning, he arrived on time, built up rapport and left. One month later he called again, this time to explore, still building rapport and recording every call on his own prospect card system.

Persisting, he called again and this time, one of our office machines had broken down. He responded quickly by showing us one of his typewriters. It's called the 'puppy dog close'. You let them hold, touch and see it. It's hard to say no!

So here we were with his machine, and ours

broken down. You guessed it — he sold, we bought.

I was talking to him after the purchase and he showed me his prospect card system. Each call carefully noted the style of buyer. He even had a number estimating how many machines he thought we would buy once he had gained our credibility. His experience suggested that you need three calls to build rapport and then to explore with up to five calls.

You need a system.

Prospect Card

Name ____________________

Address ____________________

____________ **Telephone** ____________

Type of Business ____________________

Contact Person ____________________

Buyer Requirements ____________________

____

Contact Dates __/__/__ __/__/__ __/__/__ __/__/__

A simple guide like this card system puts you in control. You know the quality of your prospect, you can decide if you intend to follow them up to get the business.

There are more sales lost than gained simply because we fail to follow-up good A and B grade buyers. That's where most of our selling time is most wisely spent.

Summing up

Get a pen and a writing pad and write your own set of questions on the basis of the special needs of your industry. Start a prospect card system to help yourself become organised and even more in control of the sales cycle. You don't need to wait until you've finished the book. Compile your list of questions right now and start using it tomorrow.

Become an explorer in the commercial jungle, because what you might discover is that your sales potential is far greater than you initially thought. Your research should open up new areas where focused, informative and controlled selling can reap far greater financial rewards with less overall time and effort.

I was recently talking with Stephen Kocizki, one of Australia's up and coming trainers, whose entire experience has come from being on the road, and he said to me, 'Exploring the clients needs by using structured questions, is the salesperson's skill of the 1990s'. He went on to say that the 'Telling method of selling is dead and active listening is a skill that we must practise.'

4 PRESENT

All right, you've done your exploring carefully, you've asked questions and you've listened. You know what the customer wants to buy, not just in a general sense but in some detail. Now it's time to present your product. It's time to make sure that your client really understands what you have to offer. It's a crucial time in the sales process. If you don't get it right you'll lose the sale. So let's see what it takes to present your product in a way that gives you the best possible chance of making a sale.

Let me start by telling you a story. Right now I'm renovating a rat-infested hovel that I bought in Sydney. It's going well. My architect has done an excellent job. The builders are great.

A few weeks ago we got to the stage where we needed a few floor tiles. About 40 square metres, in fact. A nice order for somebody. So I set off with two design consultants to spend some money.

You'd think that this was a great opportunity for a seller, wouldn't you? We knew what we wanted. We had the money and we were anxious to buy. We were a seller's dream come true. All they had to do was show us some tiles we really liked. Easy.

Here's what happened. When we walked into the first shop no-one seemed to notice us. Nobody moved. Had we walked into a taxidermists by mistake? No. It was a tile shop all right. So we helped ourselves.

We pulled out boxes, extracted tiles and blew the dust off them so we could see them properly. They had some good stock so we stuck at it, pulling and pushing. We looked under cupboards and on top of shelves and saw a lot of tiles. And we found one we really liked.

We picked up the sample and took it to the person who seemed to be in charge. He was the one who glared at us when we rattled the tiles. We tried to make eye contact.

'Excuse me,' I said, 'Is this tile suitable for both indoor and outdoor use?' For a moment nothing happened. Then his eyes fixed on the tile.

'No,' he said, 'That's just an indoor tile.' And he turned back to what he'd been doing before we'd interrupted him with our foolish question about his stock. That was it. Full stop. So we walked out again . . . for good. No sale.

The silly thing was that they had a lot of good tiles. Somewhere in that shop there probably was a tile we would have bought. But we just didn't want to do it the hard way any longer. There were other tile shops.

Off we went to the next shop. We were stiff and tired from all our pushing and lifting in the last store, so this time we went straight to a salesperson and explained what we wanted. No trouble with eye contact here. We got a steady, humourless gaze.

'Why don't you look around and see if you can find something you like?' We almost apologised for the disruption. But it sounded like more heavy work on the boxes and we weren't having any more of that. No way.

So, being smarter than the average bear, I asked if we could be shown the displays of indoor and outdoor tiles. We got another gaze. Another question. Hadn't we heard the first time?

'No, we don't have displays, but if you look over there . . .' The salesperson gave a nod of the head without breaking contact, '. . . you should find some suitable tiles.' As we left the shop I noticed a coat of arms above the door with a Latin motto. I'm not sure, but I think it said 'Service sucks'.

Okay. You know what's coming, don't you? This is where Goldilocks tries the third bowl of porridge and finds that it's just right. But there is a difference in my story. Goldilocks didn't mind having to help herself. Most buyers do.

We walked into the third shop. This looked a lot better. There were displays of tiles everywhere. And they were clearly labelled so that simple people like us would know what they were looking at. Before we had a chance to look around for a salesperson a young woman approached and smiled. She asked if she could help us in any way. So we explained the nature of our problem.

'No problem,' she said. 'How many metres of tiles do you need?' I told her.

'Well,' she said, 'where a large area of tiles is needed, some people have been using an unglazed commercial tile that is suitable for both indoor and outdoor use. In fact we have an excellent range just over there. Let me show you our display.'

She took us to another part of the shop where the tiles she wanted to show us were clearly and attractively displayed. We knew instantly that we could reach an agreement with this seller.

But it wasn't over yet. We liked the tiles, but . . .

'I wonder what this tile would look like in the sunlight?'

'Let's find out,' she said. She disappeared for a few minutes and then came back with several of the actual size tiles in the pattern we liked. Then she took us outside and placed the tiles on the ground where the sunlight could reach them. Bingo! That was the effect we wanted.

We presented her with our next problem. We liked them but we had to persuade the architect that they were right for her plans. Still no problem. 'Take the sample and show her what you've chosen,' she said. 'All I need is your name, phone number and a promise that you'll have them back to me tomorrow.'

Now that's good service. That's professional selling. She got her presentation right. So let's see exactly what she did.

1. She simplified the situation for us

She didn't present us with the full bewildering range of tiles which *might* interest us. And she certainly didn't send us off to find our own way around the shop.

Instead, she narrowed the range of options for us. She used her detailed knowledge of her stock and other customers reactions to it. On that basis she made a suggestion. She directed our attention to a tile that seemed to meet our requirements. It wouldn't have mattered if we hadn't liked it. Our reasons for rejecting it would have helped her to decide what to show us next.

She was prepared to take us on a guided tour through the items of stock which seemed potentially interesting to us. She was making it easy for us to consider the options and make a decision, because that's what a customer should be doing.

If the customer is annoyed because they have wasted their time fumbling through the stock by themselves, they won't be willing to make a decision. If they are confused by the range of choices offered, they won't be able to make a decision.

So simplify the situation. Control the presentation of options. Make it easy and focused for the customer. That's your job.

2. She showed us the product

We often make the mistake of thinking that only little children need to see and touch things in order to understand them and appreciate their possible uses. That couldn't be further from the truth. A lifetime of experience in selling has taught me that you

should never tell an adult about anything if you can show it to them instead. (Remember the 'puppy dog approach' in the last chapter.)

There are different ways of showing a product to a customer. Brochures can be useful. They can show colours and models that might not always be available in the showroom. But there is no substitute for seeing the actual product. That's the only way that it's possible to know exactly what it looks like. And that's always important. If you're buying something, like tiles, it's vital.

So, when you present your product to the customer be sure to show the product itself, if that is possible. And show it in the best possible light. In our case it was sunlight!

Of course, showing implies more than looking. If your product is a good one, your chances of making a sale increase sharply if you allow the customer to interact with the product. Looking is part of that. So is touching. And, depending on the product, hearing, smelling and even tasting might be appropriate.

Making decisions to buy requires rational thought, but it also involves the senses and the feelings. It means both knowing that the car has better fuel economy than other comparable cars; enjoying the comfort of the seats; and feeling excited about the quality of the sound from the quadraphonic stereo.

Never underestimate the importance of the irrational aspects of buying. Get your customers involved with your product. That helps them to understand what it has to offer. It also allows them to appreciate the pleasures of its use, and it will bring sales that otherwise might never have been made .

3. She helped us to solve our problems

But notice how she did it. When we expressed our concern about an aspect of the product, she didn't try to persuade us that there was nothing to worry about. The old 'Don't you worry about that' might have worked for a while for the snake-oil salesman but has no place in positive selling. Besides look what happened to the snake-oil salesman! (Seen any lately?)

What our sales expert did was to allow us to explore the problem for ourselves. As the old Chinese proverb says: 'To see is to believe, but to do is to understand'.

She took us outside so that we could see for ourselves how the tile looked in the sunlight. She created the situation. We made the judgment. She let us take the tiles to show our architect. Once again she had given us the responsibility for decision making. We were made to feel important.

It is unfortunate that selling and buying are so often seen as opposites. The seller is on one side and the buyer on the other, and a tension exists between them. Very often the buyer is made to feel inferior. It doesn't have to be that way. Look at our salesperson. She wasn't trying to manipulate us. She was trying to work with us by approaching selling as a collaborating act. Trying to ensure that we would be content with any decision we made is the best way I know to encourage a long list of happy clients.

4. She made certain that she could sustain her relationship with us

She let us take the samples away. Nice? Yes. But smart too. We had to bring them back and she had our name and phone number. When we brought the tile back we would also bring our judgment and our decision.

If it was negative she had another chance to offer us her products. If this tile wasn't suitable perhaps another one in her stock would be. While we were away she would have had time to gather together a collection of tiles which our earlier conversation would have suggested would appeal to us. This may not have been possible during our previous short visit. But now she has a focused selling group and a set presentation.

If we'd walked out without having an obligation to respond in some way, that might well have been the last she saw of us.

Your presentation should be structured to require a decision from the buyer. That doesn't mean being aggressive, but it does mean that it is reasonable to ask the buyer if they would like to purchase the product you offered. It is also okay to ask the reasons for rejection of your product. If you know what your customer doesn't want to buy you might be able to do something about it.

So don't just let them walk away. Try to sustain the contact. Offer a business card. Provide samples. Arrange for a meeting on site with your collection of samples. As long as you remain in contact, you still have a chance of making the sale.

Presenting and using brochures

When I was talking about showing your product to the customer I said that brochures can be useful. But there are two types of problems when it comes to using brochures as an aid to sales:

1. The brochures are often poorly designed.

2. We see them as junk items and salespeople rarely know how to use them.

So let's look briefly at each of these problems.

1. What are brochures for?

Does that seem a silly question? It isn't. Just go and look at some examples of brochures from almost any company you can name. In the majority of cases the brochure seems to have been reproduced to make *the company* look good, not the product or service. It's easy to imagine the General Manager and the Directors feeling warm and proud as they look at the glossy photographs of their products being used by good-looking young people in exotic settings.

But the brochure shouldn't be produced for the General Manager or the Directors, it's supposed to be for the customers, to help to sell the product. So it would probably be a good idea to give some thought to what a *customer* might expect to find in a brochure, and how it might be designed to boost sales.

Of course, I'm not suggesting that there shouldn't be glossy photographs of your product in your brochures. One of the basic functions of this type of publication is to keep your product before your customer even when they aren't in the showroom. It serves as an aid to memory and it can show other models and colours which might not be immediately available. We all know that.

But in many cases it's only the photographs that the customer looks at. The lists of features and the catalogue of technical specifications is ignored. What the customer usually wants is the answer to the question: 'If I buy your product, why should I deal with you?'

For many years it was believed that it was the product's features that sold it. But more recently the focus has changed. All the experts will tell you that the product doesn't sell itself — customers buy it. What that means is that the important thing is not the features of the product, but the customer's conviction that buying the product will bring them genuine benefits.

Brochures should not talk in terms of features, they should talk in terms of benefits and they will have even more impact if you talk in terms of advantages. They should sell the idea that the product offers the buyer advantages that purchasing similar products would not bring.

One other point must be made. Buyers won't read long passages of text. The information you give should be carefully selected to emphasise the product's benefits to the customer. It should be arranged in a format that is easy to read. Ideally it should be brief, and in point form. If the customer can't get the information in one page they almost certainly won't bother to read the brochure at all.

So, in summary, remember:

a) Keep the brochure brief.
b) Illustrate the product.
c) Focus on benefits/advantages to the customer.

2. How should a brochure be used?

Very few salespeople have any idea of what to do with a brochure. They just push a couple of their glossy, expensive publications into the customer's hands and send them out the door. That's about as bright as lighting your cigarettes with bank notes.

The basic point to remember is that when you hand your customer a brochure you cannot just *expect* them to read it. Due to your daily contact, you should be an expert on your product, so reading the brochure will be easy for you. But it might not be so easy for the customer, especially if it contains a lot of technical detail. Your job is to help customers to find the answers to their questions.

By the time you get to the brochure stage you will probably know what some of these questions will be. So get a pen or a highlighter and mark those bits of the brochure that answer these questions. Then encourage them to interact with the brochure by asking other questions so that you can help them

find that information as well and become accustomed with the brochure's style and layout.

By the time you have finished, the customer should not only know the answers to their questions, but they should be able to return to the brochure at any time and check on the information easily for themselves.

When you succeed in doing this you'll have the brochure working for you. When the customer leaves your company they should be fully adept at discussing all the product benefits to their wives/husbands/friends etc. People love to tell other people about something new.

If you are selling a service rather than a product, your strategy may have to change a little. It's commonsense that if you sell refrigerators your customers won't have trouble visualising your product. They can walk right up to it and touch it. They can open its doors, slide out its shelves and examine its meat keeper.

But if you are selling a service, it's different. The service can't be seen in the same way that a refrigerator can be seen. Your client won't be able to touch it or see how it is functioning.

To sell a service, you need to think about what that means. For example, let's look at insurance. It's an odd product. You pay for it, but there's a possibility you might never use it. And the more other people use it, the more you have to pay for it. It doesn't sound promising, does it? And yet people keep buying insurance. Why?

Because the possibility of loss by fire, theft or accident is real to them. It's part of their experience. They have had their car stolen, or they know someone who has. Aunty Sue's house was burgled last week. Their brother's house was burnt down, or their best friend's car was written off in an accident.

So they buy insurance because the inconvenience of paying the premium is outweighed by their concern about the consequences of a variety of personal disasters. Let's just go over the key points arising out of this.

1. There is a broad community awareness of insurance and its benefits, so the seller doesn't usually have to sell the idea of insurance. The agent has to sell a particular policy as opposed to competing policies offered by other companies.

2. The reason people buy insurance is because they feel the reality of the risks covered by insurance policies. They can visualise the risks and the benefits.

3. A full appreciation of the benefits of insurance comes only when you suffer a loss and have it covered by the policy which has been purchased. In other words, the service can only really be seen in action.

This is all true of other services as well. Here's a real example from another industry: radio advertising. In Wollongong, the top radio station is 2WL. They have a dynamic advertising sales team who don't just sit and wait for business to come to them. They go out into the market looking for it.

Recently the 2WL Sales Department, under the expert direction of the Sales Manager Michael Whiteman, set about attacking a problem which had arisen for them. A large local car dealer, Harrigan Ford, had stopped using radio advertising. Instead, the company had gone across to newspaper 'product and price' advertising.

So the personnel at 2WL set about planning a strategy to win back Harrigan Ford's business. This is the way they did it:

1. They involved Harrigan Ford in a research project aimed at assessing the state of the new car market. This re-established contact and gave them information about Harrigan's needs and special strengths as a company.

2. On this basis they produced sample commercials and a written proposal. In other words, they were prepared to make their services a tangible reality so the client would have no trouble understanding what was being offered.

3. They arranged a meeting with Harrigan Ford executives. At this meeting no attempt was made to close the sale. The outcomes of the research were discussed, the commercials were played and the proposal was presented. The key points of the proposal were:

a) 2WL was the number one radio station in all age-groups from 25 to 54 years old, according to the McNair Anderson ratings survey. This is important because the basic product advertisers sell is an audience. The bigger the audience, the greater the potential impact.

b) To implement an advertising strategy which consisted of spreading a small number of commercials daily over a long period of time to maximise the impact of the advertising program. This provided the client with a plan for a high impact, broad exposure attack on the market at a reasonable cost.

The strategy had been developed from what 2WL knew of the client's needs and requirements, so they knew that it was likely to be favourably received.

Once again, the printed schedule of advertisements which clearly set out the number of commercials, their distribution and overall cost helped to make their *abstract* service appear *tangible* for the client. A basis for discussion and negotiation had been established.

4. At the end of the presentation, a follow-up meeting was arranged. During this meeting several small changes were made, but the proposal was accepted in all its essential details.

The careful research done by the 2WL sales team had paid off. The Harrigan's executives did not just have to deal with the spoken word. On tape and in print the offered service was very much a visible reality. It had become the basis for further discussion and negotiation between the two parties.

And that's what you have to do too. When the client can visualise the service and consider its benefits you have a strong chance of closing the sale.

Of course, as I said before, the client will only fully appreciate the nature of your service when they experience it. So, if the reality of the service doesn't match the vision you created in your presentation, your relationship with your client will be brief. But, if you can't create that vision in the first place you won't ever get the chance to deliver the service no matter how excellent it might be.

Summing up

The way you present your product to your clients is of critical importance in the sales cycle. What you show should come from what you have learnt during the exploring phase. Your aim is to promote easy communication, and to make it simple for the customer to understand what your product has to offer them.

It is vital that any product brochures or sales material be easily understood by the customer and 'walked through' while you have the customer's attention.

If you are selling a service it is important that you do all you can to make the service appear as tangible as possible. Use printed materials, audio-visual presentations and your powers of effective communication to establish the reality of your service in the customer's mind. Then it's up to you to make sure that the delivery of the service matches the expectations you developed.

Finally, in the not too distant future, there probably won't be any sales assistants or salespeople. There will just be *customer* assistants or *customer* persons as more and more businesses realise that the customer MUST BE NUMBER ONE.

To ensure your personal success in the presentation round of the sales cycle, I suggest you follow the four simple Ss that *focus* on the customer.

The 4Ss

1. Simplify the situation.

Narrow the range of options to those that seem likely to satisfy the customer's needs.

2. Show the product in the best possible light.

Interaction with the product is important because the emotions as well as the intellect play a part in the decision to buy.

3. Solve the customer's problems.

Your aim should be to work with the customer in gaining information and making decisions.

4. Sustain your contact with the customer.

Don't just let them walk away. Do all you can to establish a reason for further contacts. As long as contact exists you have a chance of making a sale.

5 HANDLE

Objections are an important part of the sales cycle. This chapter will teach you how to handle them.

Gone are the days of the salesperson stereotype, a shifty-eyed individual with a gold tooth who will tell you anything to make a sale. What is needed is a new perspective on salespeople. We need to look at ourselves differently.

Internationally famous sales trainer, Bill Grove, best sums up today's salespeople as individuals who are 'problem solvers'. That sounds right to me! You have to think of yourself as a modern-day Sherlock Holmes, using all the available clues to uncover the truth. But what clues will you use?

One key area I've found it successful to focus on is the prospect's objections. For example:

- Their critical comments about the range of products they've seen so far.
- Their reasons for deferring a decision to buy.

The truth you can discover through 'working on' these objections is probably the only real way of finding out what is really going on in the prospect's head. Until you know what they really mean, you won't be able to find what they really want. And that means you won't sell them anything. So you need a system for dealing with the prospect's objections and using them to help you to finalise the sale. Handling objections will help you determine the right clues as to why an individual is not buying just yet.

Here's the system I've developed to recognise and deal with objections. Like all the others, it's simple and easy to follow.

1. Listen

Encourage the prospect to talk and take careful note of what is said.

2. Respond to the objection

Let your prospect know that you understand what they are saying and that you are taking them seriously. Respond with 'I see what you mean,' or 'I understand what you're getting at.'

Aim for a neutral response, free of emotion or judgment. THIS IS VERY IMPORTANT.

Try re-stating what has been said. This establishes that you have understood the objection and it gives the customer time to consider if they meant what they said.

3. Categorise the objection

Not every objection deserves a serious response. Important objections are your top priority, and need to be treated differently to the trivial or unimportant objections. You can let a trivial objection pass without any attention, but you're in trouble if you ignore important objections.

How can you tell which objections are important? Experience helps, of course, but commonsense takes you a long way. For example:

'I don't like that wallpaper in the main bedroom,' is TRIVIAL.

'I don't like the neighbourhood,' is IMPORTANT.

What's the difference? The first one can be changed. The second can't.

To overcome the first one you can suggest a simple course of action. To overcome the second you'll have to persuade them that other advantages outweigh the problem.

Above all, you have to listen closely and actively.

4. Respond promptly

When you decide that an objection deserves attention you should respond at once. If you don't, the following results might occur:

a) The prospect will concentrate on that point. They will interpret your hesitation as an indication that they're really onto something. This could make your life miserable.

b) You'll give a poor impression of yourself, if you don't give a prompt, reasonable reply to a serious objection. The prospect is likely to think that you are incompetent. That won't help the sale.

5. Deal with the objection

Once you're sure the objection is important, and you've shown the prospect that you understand what they've said, you're ready to deal with it.

The list of DOs and DON'Ts offers you a set of guiding rules for dealing effectively with the prospect's objections.

DOs	DON'Ts
Remain positive.	Be defensive and irritable.
Show interest and listen carefully.	Display indifference and boredom.
Re-phrase the objector's response.	Allow the prospect to feel that you're not taking them seriously.
Keep control of yourself and the discussion.	Talk too much or argue with the prospect.
Probe for further information with questions (e.g. Could you tell me exactly what you don't like about the bathroom?)	Try to answer irrelevent objections.
Allow the prospect to answer their own questions and find their own solutions.	Respond to objections with, 'Yes, but . . .' or interrupt the prospect.
Show how the objection is outweighed by the advantages the property offers.	Magnify the importance of the objection by overreacting.
Be precise in your response.	Hurry your response.

Use the 'feel/felt/found' method of responding

The 'feel/felt/found' method was developed to introduce another point of view in a discussion, without openly disagreeing with the prospect's point of view. For example, in reply to an objection by a prospect about using your company's accounting service, you could say,

'I understand why you feel that way. Others have felt the same, but they have found that there are special benefits in using our personalised and highly specialised accounting service.'

The 'feel/felt/found' method of dealing with an objection also has the advantage of showing how the experience of other people can help in finding solutions to the problem at hand.

6. Resolve the issue and move on

You've dealt with the objection, but is the prospect satisfied? There's no point moving on if the prospect is still uneasy about some aspect of their objection. It might become a sore point if you neglect to clear it up completely. The prospect will very quickly lose interest and only hang around out of courtesy. Everything you say will be in one ear and out the other, while they dream about what's for dinner tonight.

So don't avoid the issue. Try to focus on the precise nature of your customer's problem. You might say something like:

'I can see that you are still not certain about the price. About how much do you wish to pay?'

or

'Just suppose that wasn't a problem. Is there anything else that would stop you making a decision today?'

or

'I can see that you are still concerned about the location of this house. Could you tell me exactly what is worrying you?'

or

'You say that you are still concerned that this car is underpowered. Would you like to see some of our high performance models?'

If you confront the objection and make certain that it is dealt with properly you will save time. Even if it means that the customer decides not to buy, that is better than leaving an unresolved objection in the client's mind.

Unresolved objections become hidden barriers to a sale. So get them out of the way for better or for worse. Try to be certain that the objection has indeed been dealt with by asking:

'Does that seem all right to you?'

or

'Are you happy with that?'

Or you might try to establish agreement by repeating the customer's words.

'So what you are most interested in is . . .'

Once you're sure the customer is satisfied with your response to their objection, move on promptly. Don't return to the objection, that will just magnify its importance.

FINALLY . . . The Real Truth About Objections

In other parts of our lives, most of us have learnt that we needn't always take an objection seriously. 'No' doesn't necessarily mean 'No'. It might mean 'Maybe'. But some of us don't relate that understanding to other aspects of our lives. For example, one of the greatest problems we have in the sales process is that we tend to take objections personally. We allow ourselves to become discouraged by an objection. We can even believe that it marks the end of the deal. It has been estimated that 48 per cent of us stop the sales process when we hear the word 'No'. But we couldn't be more wrong!

Stephen Brown, who is recognised as one of the great international real estate trainers, gets it right when he says:

'The sale does not begin until the prospect says no'.

You see, many of us completely misunderstand the significance of the objection. It's not something to worry about. It's a sign that the prospect is showing real interest.

It has been said that objections are like kids in a house: If you don't hear them, you've got real problems. But, like kids again, you do need to know how to handle them properly. That's what this chapter has been all about.

Let's just briefly list the reasons why objections are a positive part of the sales process.

a) They demonstrate the buyer's interest.

b) They bring the buyer's thoughts and feelings out into the open where you can deal with them.

c) They provide you with feedback, by showing what the buyer thought you said.

d) They give you an opportunity to provide additional information or guidance.

Viewed from this perspective it should be clear to you that objections are NOT obstacles to a sale. If you deal with them properly they can help the prospect to make a decision. And whether they are positive or negative, decisions carry the selling process towards its conclusion.

Summing up

1. Objections are clues to what the buyer really needs or wants.

2. Realise that objections are a natural part of selling. Don't take them personally. They're a sign of interest. No interest . . . No reaction.

3. Remember that dealing with objections is just another aspect of communication with the client. Refer to the other chapters which deal explicitly with different aspects of communication.

4. Be a problem solver. Listen closely and, like Sherlock Holmes, use the clues on objections to help turn a negative reaction into a point of agreement. Just apply the 'feel/felt/found' system explained in this chapter. You will improve greatly with practice. It's elementary really, dear Watson.

6 TEST

It has been said that a successful seller is someone who knows their 'ABC'—'Always Be Closing'.

I see serious difficulties with this approach. The sales cycle is a lot like building a house of cards. You can put each card carefully in place and be just about finished when a tiny miscalculation causes the whole structure to collapse. And that means you have to start again . . . from the foundation card.

The real problem is that if you try to close the sale too early, or at the wrong moment, you can find yourself back where you started. You will have to re-establish rapport, explore the buyer's needs again, and so on. That isn't just irritating, it might mean that your customer's trust in you collapses. And that's the most fatal thing that can happen to a salesperson.

So let's replace the 'ABC' with 'ABT' . . . 'Always Be Testing'. This is an important distinction.

Remember that selling is an act of communication. It involves a two-way flow of information: speaking and listening. When you are selling you should keep in mind that you are really engaged in a special type of conversation with your client. And, like all other conversations, it follows a whole set of unstated rules. If you don't follow the rules you will confuse and probably offend the person you're talking to.

You don't believe me? Let me show you what I mean. Here is a situation I'm sure you'll recognise:

John: 'Hi, Kath. Do you want to meet me for lunch today?'

Kath: 'No.'

If this happens, John will probably wonder what he's done to offend Kath. He might even say something like, 'What's wrong with you?' He might be annoyed or even angry. Why should that be? All Kath said was 'No'.

The reason is that Kath broke the rules. If she was trying to keep her relationship with John open to further communication she should have said something like:

'I'd love to John, but I have an appointment with my agent.'

The unwritten rule, that no-one even thinks about, says that if you refuse an invitation, you should give a REASON. Unless you deliberately want to cause offence.

It's the same in your relationship with your customers. If you break the rules, you'll kill the relationship. Just think about it. A conversation is constructed by the people involved. They cooperate to start it and keep it going.

In most situations if you don't want to talk to

someone you don't have to. You can excuse yourself, avoid them and walk away.

It's interesting to think about the conversations you can't avoid. Such as the conversation with the police officer who pulls you over for speeding, or the conversation with the boss about the mistake that cost your company $50,000. They're not comfortable situations. And they're usually situations where one person has power over the other, or is exercising their ability to make the other person squirm.

You'd never do that? Well, let's see. Have you ever been in a situation where the other person wants to do all the talking? Or do you know any people who always use conversation to advise and direct you?

It's easy as a seller to come on too strongly: to act as the powerful person in your contact with the customer, constantly informing, advising and directing, keeping on pressing for a decision when anyone with any sense would notice that the other person just wants to escape.

So I repeat. Selling is communication. Communication is a two-way process. Good communication is a cooperative act. Make sure you allow the client to participate. Keep the dialogue open for continuation of the relationship.

You do have to close the sale. But an obsession with closing at all stages is likely to break the unstated rules of communication. This will drive the client away to someone who makes them feel that their opinions, reactions and feelings *are* of importance.

Now this is the basis for:

Feelings	Opinions	Reactions
F	**O**	**R**

Keep the dialogue open by asking for the customer's feelings, opinions and reactions.

It comes back to questioning again, but the questions will be different. You explored the client's needs through questioning. That helped you to judge what to present to them. At this stage you will want to ask questions that help the client to think things through for themselves. Your questions can bring to the surface the things that might be blocking the sale so that you can deal with them. Until the customer starts talking they mightn't even know themselves what is making them hesitate. By answering your questions they can literally talk themselves into buying.

What types of questions should you ask? Broadly you should question:

- How do you feel about this product?
- What is your opinion of its usefulness to you?
- What do you like about it?
- What do you dislike?
- What do you think?

As the conversation continues you will need to become more specific:

- How do you think it compares with competing products?
- What do you think would be the major benefits of buying this product?
- What reservations do you have about this product?

And so on.

You are testing the customer's response to the product. And as you get their answers you will know what you have to do to highlight the advantages your product will give to them. But beware! Don't keep jumping in to contradict what the customer is saying. That's breaking another golden rule. It will close communication rather than open it up. Remember to listen.

In the testing phase of the sales cycle remember your road rules:

STOP LOOK LISTEN

When you have asked the testing question, STOP.

If you LOOK back, you'll see that the questions I have suggested are all open-ended so give the customer a chance to respond fully.

While they're talking, LOOK. Attend to body language. Look at the customer's face. Take note of whether they are looking at you or at the floor. This will give you the best information about their emotional condition.

And LISTEN. Don't just hear what they're saying. Listen. Use the information they're giving you to decide what you have to do next. And feed back active interest and understanding: nod, smile, ask intelligent questions that show you understand their concerns. As John Nevin says, 'No-one has ever listened themselves out of a sale.'

Keep them talking. While they're talking, they're actually selling themselves. To keep them talking use a statement like, 'Would you expand on that, or would you take that one step further?'

Here's an illustration of the type of thing I'm talking about. Don sells computers. Not just any computers. He markets the big one — IBM. In November 1987 I let him know that I was thinking of replacing our current machines. That started the sales cycle.

But you should know that he'd been working on it before then. He'd made contact. I was aware of his product and initial rapport had been established. That's why I contacted him.

At the next stage he explored my needs. Fine, no problems there. And I liked the product. But I didn't want to buy because of the price. That didn't worry him, at least I hadn't decided to buy elsewhere. In fact, like most buyers, I was doing all I could to avoid the decision to buy. I took it to ridiculous lengths. I flew out on an overseas trip. But, before I left, Don made sure he had left room for the dialogue between us to continue. I agreed to make a decision when I returned. He had a reason to contact me. And I felt a sense of relief — out of sight, out of mind — no immediate decision had to be made.

At the end of January a new seller approached me and we went right through the sales cycle. Right down to the close. But I had an obligation to Don. I told the competitor that I would not be making a decision until I returned to Australia. That was an easy way out, more breathing space. The decision was avoided again. Don had kept himself in the event. If he'd pushed too hard it might have been different. If he'd insisted on a decision, my reluctance might have led me to say, 'Well, if it's got to be a decision now, the answer is no! It's too expensive.' End of contact.

But he'd allowed me room to move. He had a

reason to come back, and he'd kept me thinking about his product.

That doesn't mean that he left me alone. As soon as I was back in Australia, and before I'd sat on my turbo-powered, ergonomically correct, super-swivel chair at my desk, the telephone rang. It was Don.

'Hello, Doug,' he said. 'Welcome back. Are you ready to buy?'

He always beats around the bush like that. I went into an instant state of shock:my pulse rate increased. Visions of large sums of money leaving my bank account forever flashed before my eyes.

'No,' I said weakly. 'No.'

As my mind cleared I went back into the old routine.

'I'm not convinced that this is the best deal. I've seen cheaper.'

That didn't worry Don. 'Of course you can buy cheaper machines. But I'm sure that's not what you really want. We need to talk. I'll be around in ten minutes.'

You need to notice, at this point, that he could use this approach because he'd established rapport properly. A complete stranger would never get away with that. Sure enough, in ten minutes there he was. And there I was, eyeball to eyeball with him. He knew that you don't sell on the telephone. You have to be right there with the buyer. But not to intimidate, to communicate. The first thing Don did was agree with me.

'I appreciate your problem, Doug,' he said. 'IBM is more expensive than the other product you've been considering.'

But he didn't stop there. He went straight into the testing phase.

'Let's look at the competition. What exactly are they offering you? What is their range of options? What software packages can they offer that suits your needs? What backup services do they offer? How long has this company been operating? How often has it made radical changes to its basic machines?'

And then:

'How does this compare with what you know about our product?'

Don asked his questions and listened. He listened to me talking myself into the purchase. Then he had his say.

'I know you will agree, Doug, that if you buy IBM you're not just buying machines, you're buying part of the company.

'Computers need a support system and IBM provides an international support system. If we can't solve your problem in this city we'll turn to IBM Australia for their support. And if we need to, we'll go to IBM in the States. When you buy IBM you're not leaning on a dwarf. You're standing on the shoulders of a giant.

'I know that you will understand that a computer without software is useless. The greater the range of software options, the more powerful your system will be. The reason our competitors talk in terms of being IBM compatible is that we set the standards. When new software is developed, it's always developed with IBM in mind. Other companies just can't match the flexibility and range of options we offer.

'I can understand that you want to pay less. But you have to ask yourself, what will give you the best value. The competition is not the same. Ask around, anyone who knows will tell you about the quality of our product. It's reflected in the re-sale value of IBM computers.

'Sure, you can save a couple of thousand dollars now. But let me ask you: will the other company offer you the quality, the power and the support that IBM can give you? Chances are that in the lifetime of your machines, buying IBM will save you worry and inconvenience, and will offer you better trade-in values.

'So let me ask, Doug, as a businessman, is price more important than quality and service? Do you agree that IBM is offering better value than its competitors?'

It was very convincing. But making the decision was still hard. Don could see that I needed more help.

'Doug, we want your business and I know that this is right for you. I will call again at 10 am tomorrow.'

'Okay,' I said.

Don knew he had closed the sale without asking for the order. He was a long way from the old style seller pushing the contract across the desk and forcing a pen into your reluctant hands.

Let's look at what Don did in this testing phase to get the sale.

1. First let's get the basics straight. He'd done his prospecting. He'd established contact. We know about his product so that when we started to think about new computers we thought of him.

2. He'd established rapport well. We liked him personally and respected his professional approach to his work. We trusted him.

3. He'd explored our needs. He knew what we wanted and needed. And he'd put together a package which he presented to us, clearly setting out our purchasing options.

4. He'd listened to our worries and objections. And he'd talked with us about them.

5. He wasn't coming in cold. He'd been doing the work where it mattered.

But he'd come up against the most common problem of all: the buyer was reluctant to make a decision. We're all like that. What if we make the wrong decision? It might cost us a fortune. It's easier to put it aside for later. It's easier not to bring it into the open and think about it. That can cause pain. He knew that. And he knew that there were two things to be avoided above all else:

1. He had to be careful not to push too hard. I was uncomfortable, even nervous. If he insisted on a quick decision it was quite likely that I'd give him a final rejection. That was one easy way to end the mental pain.

2. On the other hand he couldn't just let me go on putting off my decision. His time was limited, he had other sales prospects to follow. A resolution has to be reached reasonably soon. So he did the humane thing. He helped put me out of my pain. And the way he did it was to guide me through the decision-making process.

Here's how it went, step by step:

1. He acknowledged that my concerns were legitimate.

   Remember, good communication is good selling. And communication will break down if you refuse to accept that the customer's concerns are genuine and deserve attention.
2. He asked questions which invited me to compare the products, but which also focused my attention on his product's strengths.

   He wasn't afraid to let me talk about his competition, but he set the agenda for the discussions by asking the right questions.

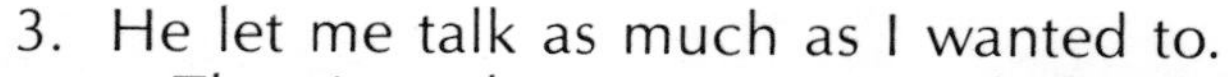

3. He let me talk as much as I wanted to.
   There's no better way to work through your problems than talking about them. Putting your thoughts into words makes things clearer.

   By answering Don's questions I made the comparisons and judgments which I had to make before I would be prepared to buy. Left to myself I would probably have avoided making the decision as long as I could, because thinking about it made me feel uncomfortable. But Don helped me to focus on the key issues so that I could make a rational judgment.

4. He responded to my concerns, building on what I had told him.
   Because I has been telling him exactly what I thought and felt about the competing products he knew just what to emphasise. He knew that I would appreciate the importance of reliability, flexibility and service, so that's what he stressed.

5. He established areas of agreement between us. He said things like:

   'I know you'll agree . . .' and 'I'm sure you understand . . .'

   And he did know. He was sure. Because he had established good rapport with me. He'd watched me carefully, and he'd listened attentively. He used his knowledge of me to point out the ways his product could match my expectations and personality.

6. Because he had set up areas of agreement it was easy for him to move towards a gentle close.
   Even now, when I had really talked myself into the sale, he knew that the best way to go was to let me make the final move. So there was no ultimatum. No heart-stopping moment of truth.

He could see that I'd got there. I'd considered the facts and made the decision. So he allowed me room to make the decision. That's smart selling.

Summing up

When you reach the testing phase of the sales cycle your job is 80 per cent done. If you've:

- Established rapport properly;
- Explored the customer's needs carefully;
- Presented purchasing options which are genuinely able to satisfy their needs;
- Dealt honestly with their objections;

then the testing phase will take you to the threshold of the sale. Only the finishing touches remain.

Remember that most people find decision-making difficult, especially when it means parting with money. Getting through this reluctance barrier is a crucial part of the sales cycle.

Your aim should be to test the customer with questions that lead them through the decision-making process, so that the final step of actually making the purchase follows easily and naturally from what has gone before.

The achievement of low stress sales should be your aim. If you model your behaviour on Don's, you will be able to sense when your customer is ready to say, 'Okay. Let's sign it up.'

Testing goes well beyond dealing with objections. Through questioning it focuses attention on the barriers to purchasing. It invites the client to talk through their problems so that the final decision is easier to make. And it is certainly true, that if you can help your customers to feel more confident about making the final decision, then sales will come more easily as well.

7 CLOSING THE SALE

A few summers ago, I took my first swimming lesson. I was shown and practised the proper Australian crawl stroke standing on the edge of the pool. Then they got me into the pool, and I blew bubbles in the water to practise breathing properly. As the lesson continued I pushed off from the edge in shallow water and floated on my face for a few metres. Finally, I was given a small board so that I could practise the correct way of kicking my legs. For half an hour my swimming instructor and I worked on the skills of swimming.

I was confident and I did everything correctly and energetically. I knew I was going to be a good swimmer.

After the lesson was over I wandered up to the deep end of the pool. I stood and looked at the water for a long time. 'I can do it,' I thought. I was wrong!

I plunged headfirst into the pool and sank like a stone. When I came up to the surface again, I was fear afloat. My arms thrashed the surface of the pool, the water level dropped noticeably as I took a long, unpleasant drink, then I went under again.

Fortunately my instructor was nearby. She dived in and hauled me out before I came to any real harm, any real physical harm anyway. My confidence took a bit of a hiding. I set myself back weeks, perhaps months, because I hadn't realised one important thing: you're not a swimmer until you can make controlled progress across the surface of the water.

It isn't enough to be a graceful stroke-maker; a powerful kicker and a great bubble blower. They're all things you have to be able to do, as part of the act of swimming. But they're not swimming. It's easy to recognise a real swimmer. If they can cross a body of water without drowning they're a swimmer. It's not a collection of isolated skills. It's a total act with a purpose.

Selling is just the same. And it's easy to recognise a seller. They are the ones who make the sales. They're not just good at rapport-building. They're not just great at exploring the client's needs, or handling objections or testing responses. They actually sell.

Like a young swimmer, a salesperson has to be able to get it all together. I said before, that most of the work is done before you get to the close. But if you don't know how to close sales, you won't be a seller. Every time you jump into the selling pool you'll be in danger of drowning. And there will be no-one there to rescue you. The lead-up is crucial. But you'll never be a seller if you don't know how to close.

So what's involved in closing a sale? It isn't easy to give a specific answer to that question. But here are some general principles:

1. Ask

It's always been a puzzle to me how some sellers can put in so much good work leading up to a sale and then lose it just because they didn't ask clearly for the client's business. Why does this happen? God knows! Maybe that's why the Good Book says, 'Ask and it shall be given unto you.' But I strongly advise you not to count on divine help. Ask for their business every time. If you don't ask you won't sell.

2. Believe

This really is starting to sound like a sermon, isn't it? But it's true. You have to believe in your product, and you have to believe that it's right for the customer. How does that sound to you? A bit unrealistic? Does it sound as if Doug's getting a bit carried away with the beauty of selling? Well think again. What I'm giving you is practical advice about effective selling. Consider this:

If you are selling a well-made product with excellent backup services, belief is easy. You know that you can offer your customers reliable solutions for their problems and satisfaction of their needs. You will be confident that each sale is right for the customer.

But, if you are selling a badly made, poorly serviced product the situation will be completely different. Each time you make a sale you will know that the customer will soon be back with problems and complaints. You'll know that the first sale to each customer will also be the last. A person who is capable of believing in a product like that is also likely to believe in the Easter Bunny and honest politicians. A poor sales record will be the least of their worries.

So find a product you can believe in. Careers aren't built on one-off sales. They develop when your customers come back to buy again and when they send other people to you because they believe the sale is right. When they do, everybody wins, everybody benefits and everybody is happy. That's the way it should be. But, if you sell an inferior product you will destroy your reputation and your career. So if you really can't believe in your product, FIND ANOTHER PRODUCT TO SELL. It's a simple matter of survival.

Before I finish this section, I have to make one thing absolutely clear. You do have to believe that the sale is right for the customer. You do have to believe that the product will solve their problems or satisfy their needs.

But you don't have to believe that your product is the only one capable of doing that. In most cases, there will be a range of excellent alternative products available to the buyer. This, in itself, can be a problem for the customer. It's great to have a choice of products. That makes it more likely that you'll find exactly what you want. But each product offers special advantages, and that's confusing. It makes it hard to decide.

As a seller your job is clear:

- You must know your product as well as you possibly can.
- You must believe in the advantages it will offer the buyer. And you must sell those advantages to them.
- You don't have to believe that your product is perfect. But you do have to believe that it has something special to offer, because that belief will come through in your presentation of yourself and

your product. Your obvious commitment to your product will generate trust in your clients, and trust sells.

So you see I was serious. Belief is basic to successful selling.

3. Concentrate

I was reading a newspaper article recently about Don Bradman. When he was smashing every batting record in the books, he agreed to have a battery of tests done on his eyes. You see, the experts were puzzled. There were other batsmen with similar techniques, and their reactions were just as quick. They concluded that Bradman must see the ball more clearly.

Guess what? Bradman's eyesight was perfect. But it was no better than the other batsmen's vision. So what made him better? His wife knew. She said that Bradman's game started the moment he got up on the day of a match. He started concentrating then.

He was great because he gave absolute attention to each delivery. His powers of concentration meant that he didn't miss any significant information as the bowler ran towards him and as the ball swung through the air. He was always able to play a shot which was a response to what was really happening, not to what he thought might happen.

Bradman's technique was great. He had all the skills, and he certainly understood the game he was playing. But he knew that to be better than the others, he could never take anything for granted. He had to respond to the exact circumstances of the moment, and that required intense concentration, especially on the bowler and the ball. He had to read all the signs and respond appropriately if he wanted to succeed.

Closing a sale is the same. I've already said that selling is an act of communication. Communication also requires concentration so that you can respond appropriately to the special circumstances of the moment. You have to listen and watch closely so that you can respond to the person, and the context. If you can do that well you'll be a cut above the rest, like Don Bradman. But it's also the reason why I can't give you simple directions for what you should do to close a sale.

I will give you some examples of different ways to close a sale. But remember that, in the real world, little things can change the way things are going. You have to concentrate and respond to what is happening, not to what might happen. For example, things might be going really well but suddenly your customer begins to feel ill because he had too much to eat for lunch, or perhaps you said something that made him feel uncomfortable.

The point is that you are dealing with human beings, not machines. And human beings vary from one moment to the next in the way they respond to people and circumstances. If you want to be a seller who is a cut above the rest you will have to become an expert at concentration and response. Keep that in mind as you read the following suggestions.

4. Evaluate

All right. You've concentrated. You've listened. You've watched. If you've really done those things, you will know when your client feels all their problems and questions have been dealt with and answered. You'll know from the things they say that they have reached a point where they agree that your product seems right for them. That's the moment when you should move to close the sale. If you leave it hanging, even for a little while, the mood might change and the sale could be lost.

Closing a sale can be that delicate. Move too soon and you can make the customer cautious and resistant. Leave it too long and you might lose the sale to someone else. You just have to learn to respond sensitively to what's happening.

You should also be making an evaluation of the type of person you're dealing with. Good sellers are good observers of human beings. They learn to recognise personality types and the types of approaches which suit each type. Let me give you a few examples of different types of closes and the people they suit.

a) Direct close

I bought my last car from a salesman named Charlie Gall. He'd done it all properly: established rapport, explored my needs, presented his product well, handled my objections and tested my responses. And all the time he'd been watching me and listening to me. He'd made an assessment of my personality. He knew that I wouldn't be nervous about making a decision. He knew that I didn't have to feel that I was running things. And he knew that I was a businessman, and that in today's business world we don't really buy anything any more. We just authorise or approve things.

He also knew that he'd sold me the car. He could tell from my responses. But he had to secure the sale. So what did he do? He moved directly to close the sale.

'All right Doug,' he said, 'it's clear that this is just the car you've been looking for. Why don't you let me take care of the details and you can come in tomorrow and drive it away?'

It was the right approach, for the right person, at the right moment. So I approved the purchase and Charlie handled the details. Bingo! It was all over. The sale was made.

b) Alternative choice close

Charlie got it right with me, but the same approach with someone else might not have worked as well. Some people have to feel that they are in absolute control. If the seller is too direct they become suspicious and even hostile. With people like that you have to be sure that they feel that the final decision is theirs and theirs alone. So, when the moment is right, you have to create a situation in which the client can make a decision which is clearly their own. No pressure. No manipulation. It might go something like this:

'All right, madam. We've looked at a number of products which will solve your problems. They are all excellent value for money. Which one do you believe is right for you?'

Remember that you have to be like a barrister in court. *Never ask a question unless you know the answer you're going to get.* If you move too soon your client might say, 'None of them.' But if you've done your preparation work properly, and listened closely so that the move is well timed, this type of close will allow your customer to feel in control. It will permit them to make their own decision to buy, or not to buy.

Whatever the result, trying to match your approach to the client's personality will improve your chances of success.

c) Summary close

What about the type who likes to consider all the facts and pride themselves on making logical decisions? You know, the one who takes home every booklet and pamphlet you are able to give them. They like to show that they know as much about your product as you do. That's good. Go with them. Give them as much information as they want. Discuss the product with them, highlighting the advantages it will give them. When you sense that the moment is right, summarise the facts, emphasising the aspects of the product which most interested them. Then, ask for the sale.

If you've presented the facts clearly and logically, they'll probably buy. Not just because the product is what they want, but because they will feel reassured by a style of presentation that matches their own way of thinking.

It is impossible to cover all the variations you might meet in selling situations and to suggest specific ways of dealing with each one. As I said earlier, the key to successful closing is a sensitive response to the person and the situation.

The examples I have just given illustrate the things you might do. But it's up to you to use the principles I've outlined. So go to it and learn to close a sale in the way you learn everything else, from experience.

d) Double close

What's a double close? Let me explain by sharing a story with you.

At one stage I was involved in the purchase of a property through a seller named Lynn. On this occasion I was a nervous buyer. I wasn't at all sure that the purchase was right for me. But Lynn believed that I was getting exactly what I wanted. At no stage did she falter in her belief, and her conviction that the sale was right carried me along.

I made an offer which was accepted. But doubts lingered on. We all fear that the worst will happen. We hate making decisions and we worry about them after they've been made. That's the state I was in when I entered her office to pay the deposit.

As soon as Lynn saw me, and before the cheque was drawn, she looked directly at me and said, 'Doug, don't worry about the property or the price. It was right for you. You've done well.' And I believed her because I could feel her genuine conviction. The strength of her belief convinced me that I had done the right thing.

That's the double close. It consists of a simple reassurance to the buyer that they have made a good purchase. It is an important final step in the sales cycle. Use it. But only if you really believe that the customer has done well. Insincerity is transparent and can make a contented buyer nervous once more.

Summing up

It should be very clear by now that if you can't close, you can't sell. Closing is an art. It is listening, talking, observing and being ready above all to ask for their business as you near the end of the sales cycle. If you have carefully followed the steps of the cycle it should be almost automatic.

The key is to listen for the buying signals your client is giving out: a statement, a gesture, a nod. The clue can be verbal or nonverbal. It's up to us to identify these signals. Once identified, don't be afraid to move straight into the close. We have just discussed some of the broad range of closes possible. With experience you will learn to match the right close to each individual customer.

Although we've reached the end of another chapter, I just want to make the point that 'closing' a sale is really the *start* of more sales. Usually, when we talk about 'closing' something, we mean that we've finished or shut it down. We close bank accounts, we close fetes and exhibitions, we close our eyes and shut out the light. But closing a sale is different. It's part of the sales cycle, and cycles keep going around endlessly, like a merry-go-round. Closing a sale is a dynamic act. It opens things up and keeps the carousel turning. It must not shut them down.

When we talk about 'closing' a sale, we need to think of it as being like completing an electrical circuit by throwing a switch. When you press the switch, a gap closes and the current starts to flow through the circuit. Closing the switch energises the circuit into new activity. That's what happens when we close a sale. Money and goods or services change hands. Relationships are formed. The new product opens up fresh possibilities for the buyer and seller.

The new business relationship adds another segment to the growing network of contacts for the seller. So it's very important that when you do close a sale you shouldn't think, 'Well, that's another one finished'. Instead you should think, 'Well, that's something else started. Let's see what can be built on that foundation.'

8 AFTER-SALES SERVICE

There are many reasons why some sellers are more successful than others. I've discussed some of them in this book. One of the things that really singles out the superior seller is the quality of their after-sales service.

'After-sales service?' you say. 'That's not selling, and anyway it only applies to new cars.' Wrong! And wrong again! After-sales service has a great deal to do with our success as sellers. And it applies to everything that can be sold.

I've said it before, but that's not going to stop me saying it again. Your sales career will be secure when your customers keep coming back to buy again. It will flourish ONLY when they refer their friends and business contacts to you.

So your career will rest on those two Rs:

- Return Sales
- Referrals

Good after-sales service contributes to the development of both.

Think of it like this: Making a sale establishes a relationship. If they bought from you, they probably trust you. It would be stupid to let them forget you, especially when it takes only a little effort and organisation to maintain contact.

Let me tell you a couple of stories which show how it can be done. When I decided I needed a car telephone I was referred to a young man called John Clarke. He was well organised and efficient with a strong self-image. We did business: I bought, he sold — and I had a car telephone. End of contact? Certainly not!

One week later my telephone rang. I picked it up.

'Doug?'

'Yes,' I said.

'It's John Clarke.' Good God, I thought, I can't have paid the bill. But I said, 'Yes, John. How can I help you?'

'I'm just ringing to see whether everything is okay with the phone. Any problems?'

'No,' I said. 'It's fantastic.'

'I'm pleased to hear that,' he said. 'Don't hesitate to contact me if you need help.'

That's nice, I thought. And unusual.

End of contact now? No, again. Three months later I received a brochure from him about a new product he was selling. Then, five months after that, he rang me again to tell me that he'd changed companies.

He knew that successful selling depends on establishing and maintaining good business relationships. So he was letting me know where I could find him.

You can be sure that when I need the type of product John sells I will contact him. You can also be sure that I told all my friends about him. Now, I don't know how many of my friends actually contacted John, and I don't know if he sold anything to any of them. But I do know that professional communicators who service their clients consistently and efficiently get results. I feel confident that John will make more sales every year because he makes an effort to provide after-sales service. He systematically maintains the business relationships he has formed.

Here's another example: Marie Davis is a real estate agent. She's a very effective and successful seller. But she doesn't sell and forget. Six to eight weeks after each sale, the buyer will hear the front doorbell ring. When they answer, there's Marie on the doorstep. She's not afraid to hear that the roof leaks or that the cockroaches have kidnapped the family cat and are asking for ransom. She really wants to solve any problems that might have occurred. And that attitude keeps business relationships solidly glued. It shouldn't surprise you to know that a lot of her clients keep coming back.

In general, after-sales service is really commonsense and should become second nature to any salesperson. It is the key to a long life in selling. Walt Disney said years ago that he wanted to create such an exciting park that when people would visit, they'd have such a good time they would always come back. And, when they did come back, they would bring their friends with them. In other words, make your client a walking, talking public relations consultant for you.

Let's look at another more personal example.

Those of you who know me, realise that I take a size 11EEE shoe to house my flatfeet. The army is not for me. Now, just to keep walking, I wear soft-sole shoes. My minders tell me they look dreadful and I should clean up my act. But at fifty years of age, there is not much left to clean up, so I wear comfortable shoes.

The company that has these shoes is the Floorshine Shoe Company. Here's what happened when I visited the store.

'Good morning sir.' I was greeted.

'Yes, I am looking for size 11EEE in walking shoes.'

'Certainly sir.' The sales attendant brought three boxes, 'I think one of these styles will suit you.' He opened the first box and started the presenting phase.

'How does that seem?' he enquired.

'Great,' I said.

'This is a new style,' he enthused, opening up another box. 'Let's try one of these as well.'

Now that is cross selling at its best. I had given the buying signals. Not prepared to settle for the sale of one pair of shoes he went for two.

'Do you take American Express?' I asked.

'We certainly do,' he exclaimed.

When packing up my shoes he queried, 'Can I assist with socks or polish?'

'Not at this stage,' I replied.

Not deterred by a rejection he asked, 'Mr Malouf', (he now had my name from the American Express Card), 'Would you care to fill out this form for our records?' He handed me a form, it looked simple enough, so I thought why not. All completed, big feet exits, goes home and forgets the whole transaction.

Six weeks later across my desk was a letter welcoming me to the Floorshine Shoe Company VIP club. Six weeks after that I had my very own VIP card.

What are they doing? Marketing of course. They are getting me ready for the next purchase via after-sales service. Repeat business is the best business. Why you say? Well, the trust is in place. Once you have that trust, why lose it? US studies show that it takes *ten* more prospective customers to create a *new* buying customer, than it does to keep an old one. It is critical to water your established client base.

Remember that with prospecting you are prospecting for new business, but with after-sales service you are *protecting* it!

Have you ever been to Hong Kong and purchased anything? They are masters of the after-sales service phase! Buy something anywhere and you will be on a mailing list forever. In fact I was there way back in 1971. I can't even remember if I bought anything, but every year I still receive a Christmas Card with my name on it.

To be successful at after-sales service you need to set up a system where the people who have bought from you, hear from you again and again. There are a number of inexpensive ways to maintain contact and trust. For example:

- Write a letter.
- Call in and say hi.
- Telephone to see how the product/service is going.
- Send something like the latest brochure in the mail.
- Send out Christmas/Easter/Birthday cards.
- You may want to buy yourself some small give away item to keep your client base stimulated.

I am big on key rings and have been using them in my training sessions as client give aways for five years. They are spread all over Australia, New Zealand and America. I can't say that I am winning because there are over 4000 key rings floating around out there. However, I can say with confidence that 90 per cent of my consultancy work comes from referrals, and these key rings serve as a constant reminder of my whereabouts. My business and client cards are also out there working for me.

Summing up

After-sales service means looking after your client's needs and solving their problems after the point of sale. It means that you consider the service to be part of the product; not just selling an insurance policy, but also making sure that claims are processed and paid promptly. It means not just shampooing carpets but also putting the furniture back exactly where it came from, and telephoning the next day to see if the customer is happy with the job. It means not just selling computers, but also calling regularly to see if you can help to solve any problems that may have arisen.

If any of this sounds ridiculous or unreasonable, I suggest that you take a close, critical look at your ideas of what selling and service really mean. You should begin by asking yourself these questions:

- Do you maintain communication with your clients after the sale?
- Do you contact your past buyers at least twice a year?
- Do you have a system you follow for maintaining the contacts you have established through the sales you have made?

- Do you believe that solving problems connected with your product after the sale is just as important as solving problems before the sale?
- Do you regard after-sales service as part of your product rather than an optional extra?

If your answer to any of these questions is 'No' then you need to change your ways of operating so that you can honestly answer 'Yes' instead.

Remember what Mae West said: 'If you don't use it, you lose it.' Now, she wasn't talking about selling, well not directly anyway, but it is true of selling just the same.

If you don't make a deliberate attempt to sustain your relationships with past buyers you'll lose them. And that should be a matter of serious concern to you. If you don't maintain the old contacts while you make new ones, there will be no growth and development in your career. The sales merry-go-round will come to a halt to the disappointment of yourself and the customers that have ridden with you to date.

So remember — after-sales service isn't just an optional extra, it has to be an essential part of your approach to selling if you truly want to succeed.

9 MMMM... SOME FINAL ADVICE

It's been a long, fun ride on the sales merry-go-round, hasn't it? But I'm hungry, aren't you ? What we need now is some final advice that you can really sink your teeth into. I wonder who you could have lunch with? Let's consider the prospects: your mum, a friend, a successful salesperson, a politician or your main buyer perhaps. Which one would you choose? Let's see if I can influence your choice in this chapter.

Throughout this book I've talked about my selling/buying experiences and various ways to improve yourself and your selling techniques. But it's not only selling guides, a conservative haircut or a 'whiteboard' that make the difference — it is *you*.

For selling to be a cinch you have to find a way to make yourself change your attitude and enthusiasm to the selling you do. The best way to do this is to find a mentor. Someone you can look up to, and yet relate too. Ask yourself who in your local community or line of business would you most like to emulate. Then, take a simple positive step. Call them! Or write to them! All you have to say is that you would like to meet them or buy them lunch.

Be honest about your motivation with them. Tell them you are looking for encouragement and direction and remember — the real movers and shakers have no difficulty in sharing their knowledge. Chances are, they have been where you and I are and somebody helped them get started. One of the most sought after rewards of entrepreneurs is not just money, but recognition. You will be providing this reward at very little cost. At the very worst, all you will be giving up is the cost of a telephone call.

On the positive side, you might be starting a relationship or a network of contacts that may change your selling life forever. You see, a mentor has one great asset to share — 'sales experience'. Anyone that has 'been there, done that, sold that' is always one step ahead of you. Talking to such people makes your thoughts or dreams of what you think you could do, appear more real. Quite simply, associating with a mentor can quicken your ride on the sales merry-go-round.

Now, taking a mentor to lunch is not just an excuse to try and impress someone or try out a new restaurant. In speaking (but mainly listening) to a mentor, four major concerns will more than likely be raised which the 'experienced one' has found to be of most benefit over the years.

Having spoken with numerous successful individuals in the selling profession myself I've classified these as the 4Ms or MMMM:

1. Adopt a positive Mindset
2. Make a decision that school is never out
3. Make a yearly personal goal for what you're selling
4. Make yourself do the things you don't want to do

1. Catch a positive mindset

Before you sit down to look at the menu, the first thing that should strike you about the person you're dining with is their positive attitude mindset to everything. Otherwise you've picked the wrong mentor. The menu will 'look great'. Another positive remark like 'Isn't the colour scheme in the restaurant attractive?' will be enthused.

What's the advantage to you? A positive mindset is as contagious as the flu. So drop your immune system and try to catch it. After you've parted company, think back on that feeling of being with a positive person. Try to capture it and relive it. Try it on your friends. After a little practice you'll think you're spreading the plague. Then try it on your buyers/prospects. After all, it's more sales that we're after.

2. Make sure that school's never out

Your mentor might tell you about the 'school of hard knocks' which is unfortunately a part of selling life. You may learn or educate yourself to be wary of such events, but don't waste valuable time worrying about whether or not those knocks are going to happen. Talk about and find out more on how your mentor keeps up-to-date with their business. This may range from reading the latest books on improving your selling techniques (like this one), to taking on a part-time post-graduate marketing degree.

The golden rule is 'never stop trying to educate yourself'. Also be aware that there is no need to stop at learning from just one mentor. Remember, that even mentors who don't keep up-to-date quickly fall behind to the back of the pack, regardless of past successes.

3. Make a personal yearly sales goal

Successful people rarely make it by accident. Planning how to achieve a particular goal has always been a critical part of success. Mentors will tell you this, sales books, and textbooks will tell you the same. Plan this, write down that, collect this first, do that.

What I feel is important, is to be *specific* and *personalise* your sales goal. Think in terms of what size sales goal you can reasonably achieve through the ensuing year. Then up it by 10 per cent, just to make your goal worth striving for. This goal should be clearly displayed on your 'whiteboard'. As each month passes draw up a quick bar graph to show your sales progress. This will serve as a constant reminder of what you have achieved. And remember, set a specific goal based on your sales experience to date.

4. Make yourself do the things you don't want to do

Remember as children we always had to eat our vegetables before we even looked like getting sweets? Well, I know this is a luncheon meeting, but the principle is the same. You've got to find that something special in you to make yourself do the things you don't want to do.

When I was at school, all the other kids could swing completely around the monkey bars. They all looked very clever, but I couldn't do it. I was scared.

I just didn't want to do it. I guess this was one of my first tests of personal courage and motivation. Despite the daily lunchtime peer pressure, I valiantly resisted. My heart just wasn't in it, but I knew I had to change. I finally told my older brother about this and although he laughed at first, he took me down to the playground after school when my teasing friends weren't there. He quickly showed me how easy it was. It was all technique.

The point is, that apart from listening to someone more experienced than I (a mentor), I had made myself do something I really didn't want to do by adopting the right technique. It could just as well have been a new selling technique or system I hadn't read or heard about before.

Talk to anybody. No matter how successful they are, they will all dislike doing one thing or another. However, there is usually a difference. They don't let it put them off. They've usually found a way or technique to conquer and do the things they don't like to do. This makes their daily life much more productive and clears their mind quickly and effectively from thinking about less pleasant concerns. The less clogged the mind, the easier the fun tasks in life can be accomplished and enjoyed.

Don't put unpleasant tasks off, get rid of them. For example, you may have a client who you don't like. Although you should call on them, you keep putting it off week after week. For all you know they could easily become one of your major buyers. Find a technique for getting over the problem. Remind yourself of the potential importance of this person to you.

Even little tasks, like getting into a habit of writing a daily 'TO DO' list may be a proverbial pain in the neck. But, you must take the bad with the good, and not put them off. All we've really talked about in this chapter is having lunch with a mentor to change our personal attitude to selling. There is nothing more simple to do than eating, is there?

We've just used the everyday event of eating as a way or means of showing you how to ride the sales merry-go-round with a little more conviction. Learning from a mentor is just another tool to add to your collection of selling techniques and strategies described in this book. It can, however, be one of the most valuable learning activities to be taken. It's a little bit like graduating to the inside circle of horses on the merry-go-round, where the sales cycle seems to go by more quickly.

By seeing and hearing how others have 'been there, done that, sold that' you can take steps to:

- Adopt a positive Mindset.
- Make a decision to continually educate yourself.
- Make a personalised yearly sales goal.
- Make yourself do the things you don't want to do.

Remember, there are no short cuts to completing the sales cycle. To try a short cut is a bit like trying to cut straight across a rotating carousel. Chances are you'll end up right back where you started from with no sale made. Practise going through each of the eight steps of the sales cycle we have discussed in this book for effective selling. Utilise the various sales techniques described, and as experience comes your way, you will become the show pony of the sales merry-go-round. Selling really will become a CINCH!

INDEX

Meet the team who wrote the book:

Cragmar Centre
Princes Highway
WOLLONGONG NSW 2500
Tel: (042) 29 8244
Fax: (042) 27 2545